Contact Centre Team Management
A Practical Guide

Kenny Gow

Copyright © 2021 Kenny Gow

All rights reserved. No part of this publication may be reproduced, stored in a retrieval system or transmitted, in any form, or by any means, without the prior written consent of the author, nor be otherwise circulated in any form of binding or cover other than that in which it is published and without a similar condition being imposed on the purchaser.

DEDICATION

To Ann and Jenny

CONTENTS

	Acknowledgments	i
	Introduction	1
1	What Does A Team Manager Actually Do?	5
2	Coaching	43
3	Building Engagement	51
4	Performance Management	63
5	HR Related Things	71
6	Putting It All Together	91
7	Summary	105
8	Terminology	107

ACKNOWLEDGMENTS

Thank you to all my contact centre colleagues, past and present, for their support and friendship. In particular: David McInally, Paul Moore, Carl Schaefer, Duncan Stevenson, John McLuskie, Alan Stark, Anthony Simpson, Gary Irvine, Craig Brodie and countless others.

INTRODUCTION

This is not an academic-style text book. You won't find any management theory in these pages. No mention of Maslow, Denning, Fayol or even Drucker...though it will do you no harm at all to get a basic grasp of what these people have added to the development of management science over the years. What you'll find between these covers is a simple, practical and easy to understand guide to successfully managing the everyday challenges of the Team Manager role in contemporary contact centres.

This short book is intended to provide anyone who works in the contact centre industry with an understanding of how to develop the practical skills and characteristics necessary to become a competent, capable and respected Team Manager.

I've tried to make it easy for the reader by breaking the role down into a series of distinct bite-sized learning chunks covering each of the core capabilities expected of a first-class people manager. I'll take you through the fundamentals of how to build your practical expertise in each area and offer up a series of observations to allow you to consider how to put theory into practice in 'real world' situations.

I like to simplify processes, activities and instructions into five points or less. I firmly believe that looking after the top five or so key priorities in most situations will allow almost anyone to absorb the majority of what's required to succeed in any role. For example, let's train new agents to be competent in the five most common call types then they will feel confident in handling nine out of ten calls presented to them. The gaps in knowledge can be closed through floor support and coaching. They really don't need to be confused by the small stuff at the start of their careers and will be in a better place to pick up the detail as they progress if they have a decent understanding of those five most common call types and familiarity with what they sound like.

At various points I've listed a bunch of key messages or 'take-aways'. If you absorb nothing else from the book then please, please think about the points I make in these sections. I promise you that what's included is a little bit of concentrated wisdom. This has been built up over twenty-five years in contact centre management and may just deliver for you the kinds of tips, hacks and shortcuts that could save you unnecessary time and pain as you begin your career in management.

Most importantly, this is a book of *practical* information designed to run alongside any formal management education you may receive from your employer or at college or university. You won't find any management theory or science in these pages – I have decided to concentrate solely on the myriad of day to day issues and challenges that new, inexperienced or overwhelmed managers may face during the early stages in their new roles. I want readers to learn both what to expect and how to deal with or prevent the most challenging situations as they become apparent.

Get your highlighter pen ready to colour every phrase, sentence or paragraph that may help you deal with specific problems and difficulties as they become real to you.

Finally, a gentle word of warning. From this point on I write as I speak. Please don't get on your high horse about dubious grammar and split infinitives. The casual, informal and honest style is deliberate and my plain speaking is designed to help you, the reader, appreciate as many of the challenges and intricacies of the contact centre TM role as possible. I want to leave you with a very clear picture of what is required to succeed and how to avoid the many pitfalls.

I'll sometimes refer to Team Managers as TMs or just 'managers' and I often like to use capitals at the beginning of the title – don't know why, it's just a habit. I'll also talk about agents, advisers, CSAs, call handlers, your people, direct reports etc. They all mean the same thing; someone who handles phone/chat/social media conversations in a contact centre environment for a living. They may be a 'she' or a 'he' and nothing should be inferred from my use of these…..I'm just trying to avoid too much repetition and I don't want to bore either the reader or the writer (me).

Don't forget, contact centres are fun, noisy, dynamic places to work. A capable and sensitive Team Manager can make life great for their team members while building a fulfilling and rewarding career for themselves. Aspire to be that manager. The information in this book will support you in taking your first steps on what should be an amazing journey.

1 WHAT DOES A TEAM MANAGER DO?

When performed properly, the TM role is one of the most complex and demanding in any contact centre. The expectation is that a fully competent Team Manager will have knowledge and skills in all of the following areas…..please bear in mind that this list is not exhaustive and you could easily add half a dozen or more functions in which you'll be expected to perform well:

- Coaching
- IT and Reporting
- Human Resource Management
- Material Resource Management
- Real-Time Management
- Floor Support
- Recruitment
- Training
- Quality Monitoring and Improvement
- Compliance
- Health and Safety
- Motivation
- Sales
- Leadership
- Operations Management
- Performance Management
- Customer Service
- Facilitating Meetings

- Being Nice To People You Don't Especially Like
- Making Your Insecure Bosses Feel Good About Themselves

Okay, that last two are a little bit tongue in cheek but don't be surprised at the range of things you – as a Team Manager – will be expected to 'just get on with' as part of your daily routine. From fire drills to finding someone's missing chair back support to counselling a recently bereaved team member to preparing evidence to support an employee's potential dismissal…..it's all on you! And all of this while doing the day job of hitting targets and keeping your line manager happy.

Please don't underestimate the breadth and complexity of the TM role.

However, don't despair - help is at hand. Let me show you how to organise and prioritise your workload in a way that will stop you from feeling overwhelmed and will allow you to become so well-known for your effectiveness that complete strangers will be competing to sit beside you in the cafeteria at lunchtime to tap your brain and garland you with what should feel like undeserved praised.

Where To Start

I'm biased. As a pretty typical contact centre manager I expect you to hit all of your numbers without any fuss, be great to your people and make yourself available to support me with a myriad of small projects that I'll be only too keen to delegate to you. I don't want to have to clear up any mess you have made by upsetting other departments, clients, customers or staff. In short, I need you to make my life as easy as possible as it's very likely that I'll be kept pretty busy doing all the things my boss expects of me. I don't want you dropping any unexpected and unwanted surprises on me.

To help you get started I'm going to list five basic but fundamental areas which you should focus on and which will become the pillars of your activity as a Team Manager. Fill your time pursuing success in these and you won't go far wrong.

1. Achieve Daily/Weekly/Monthly Targets.
2. Performance Management.
3. Coaching and Development.
4. HR Responsibilities Including Managing Absence and Attrition
5. Floor Support – Making Yourself Available To Your Team.

I'm so keen that this becomes your list of top priorities that I've repeatedly covered each throughout the book – sometimes repeating the same highly important messages. I promise you this - if you become expert in pillars 1-5 and put in the required time and effort applying that expertise with your people you will make a success of the TM role. You will also soon learn that, to some extent, each of the five priorities feeds into the others – in short it all joins up and a smooth 'joined-up' approach to managing your team is what you should be aiming for as opposed to a disjointed, staccato, chaotic mess. When chaos prevails agents often don't really know what's expected of them from day-to-day and, as a result, feel insecure in the role and assume the characteristics and mindset of temporary staff who can feel like they are simply 'passing through'.

What's next then? Well, take away the top five and you're left with a bunch of key activities that you should spend any free time you may have getting to understand more about. Then learn to apply them within the daily 'business as usual' (BAU) agenda as and when they become appropriate. What follows is a series of short notes designed to offer some background information on what each entails, how to apply within a contact centre setting and where to learn more.

Technology

Call centre staff lose, break and make a mess of their hardware all the time. It's amazing how much time can be wasted having to deal with a missing headset or mouse or a keyboard that someone appears to have eaten their breakfast off of. How often do new staff forget their logins or get themselves locked out of the network because they've used up their three shots at inputting a password correctly? Why does all of this always seem to happen first thing in the morning on the busiest day of the week when no-one is available to help you find spare hardware or re-set logins ?

Here's a fundamental truth for you – these things will always happen and you can never prevent them occurring from time to time. So, how can you stop this becoming a daily or weekly circus at the start of shifts at key times of the day? Simple – planning and preparation.

First, take the time to learn everything there is to know about how the kit on each workstation fits together. By simply knowing where cables attach and how it all functions can save time on unnecessary Tech Support tickets. Tech guys don't like you fiddling with their gear but seem to get equally annoyed if you've called them out just to shove a lead into the back of a monitor. You can't really win in these situations other than to do whatever it takes to get your people live and available as soon as you can without destroying expensive equipment.

Second, anything that's under the control of an agent must become their accountability. If each person is responsible for bringing their headset to work or storing in a safe place within the building then it must be made plain that it's part of the expectations around the role to be logged in with their headset on ready to take calls five minutes before their shift begins (it helps if this is covered off at recruitment and new agent induction training stages to avoid any 'misunderstandings' when people first go on line). This allows for any minor issues to be dealt with before calls begin to be delivered at the start of the agreed shift time. Forgotten passwords or headsets left at home cannot be allowed to delay the start to the working day.

Here's where the planning and prep comes in – go round all desks at the end of the day and the beginning of the next to see if anything obvious is missing. Make sure you have a source of spare headsets, keyboards and mice. It's easy to get annoyed with the guys who cause you problems like this on a regular basis but you can deal with the serial offenders when everyone is a little less busy. The start of any shift is not a great time to begin this kind of discussion with wayward advisers. Get them logged in and handling customer interactions as soon as you can.

Also, at the end of every agent's shift, light-heartedly remind them to guarantee that they will remember their headset, login and password at the start of next day's work. Hammer it into them until it becomes a cardinal sin to turn up to work without the correct equipment and appropriate logins/passwords.

Third, keep an up to date password protected spreadsheet of everyone's logins (not passwords as they should be private, personal and secure). Have direct line numbers for two people within the team responsible for setting up and re-setting system/network logins and passwords. Build great relationships with these guys as they can make or break your day if it starts in login or password chaos. Remember, don't try to take a shortcut by sharing your login or that of an existing or former member of staff as this will almost certainly be a breach of security.

Don't be afraid of contact centre technology. Dive in and learn all there is to know about how it works and how you can make it work for you and your team. For example, teach yourself how to legitimately access any printer or copier in the building and save yourself the frequent panic of not being able to meet a reporting deadline because your favourite printer is down. Buy a friendly Tech Support person a couple of drinks on a Friday after work and get them to share some of their knowledge, shortcuts and hacks – you never know, they might also start to prioritise your support requests over the grumpy, self-obsessed, uninterested TM blokes who like to give the impression that IT Support people are geeky, gaming obsessed freaks with personal hygiene issues.

Develop strong, friendly relationships with support functions and your life will become an awful lot easier.

Applications and Systems

You really don't have to become an expert user of all the applications you'll be expected to use during your time as a Team Manager but I would recommend that you develop above average skills in the following.

To be able to fully support your team and demonstrate a high level of capability within your role you will have to have a clear insight into the workings of your proprietary customer manager system (CMS). This is the application that advisers use to manage your business's relationship with its customers. They're usually given random names like 'Buddy' or 'Sherlock' or an acronym containing the first letters of the full technical title; something along the lines of '**E**nergy **D**ivision **C**ustomer **F**ile' (shortened to EDCF) or similar. No matter what they're called you will have to know the workings inside out and be able to educate and coach your people on how to use it more efficiently.

The CMS is where almost all of an agent's day-to-day work will be done. On this platform they will take payments, send bills, record sales information, change names and addresses and make notes on the reason for the customer's call and what action was taken. These applications invariably do an awful lot more than these few basic tasks and it's imperative that you learn just what exactly they are capable of while building a vocabulary of navigation and function shortcuts. Let me give you a word of advice that will stand you in very good stead:

*xpert in the workings of your CMS than the most
[adv]iser on the call floor.*

Nothing will bring you more respect with your team members than being able to handle all their system queries and show them how to better navigate through it. The corollary of this is also true. Nothing loses respect for a TM with an agent quicker than him being unable to give them authoritative live support when dealing with a complex CMS related enquiry. Running off to look for a more capable manager to help you out is really not a good look and delivers poor service to any caller having to wait on the line longer than expected because of your lack of knowledge.

Often your first TM job will be in a department or on a campaign that you are unfamiliar with. You may even be seconded into an area you know absolutely nothing about and have had no basic training for. This must not become an excuse and you should make every effort possible to learn the appropriate CMS in your own time – even if this means putting in hours of unpaid overtime and buddying with more experienced TMs or senior advisers in an effort to pick up everything they know. It will feel awkward to begin with but will pay dividends very soon as you become a capable and trusted colleague. Failure to get to grips with the system early will leave you dreading hands going up as agents require your support and leave you feeling foolish and mildly incapable during your time on the project.

The ability to access recordings of all customer interactions, whether that be voice, social media, chat, video etc., is crucial to managing quality and compliance standards within your team. Nothing will tell you more about the performance of an individual customer service agent than monitoring their activity at the more stressed or inconvenient points in their working days and week. As an example, when I was a contact centre manager in a voice setting, on return to the centre on a Monday morning, I would arrange a call listening session with a small number of Team Managers during which we would select a bunch of recordings of their agents taken from the period on Friday at 8pm until close of play on Sunday. I would prioritise very long or short calls handled at the end and start of peoples' shifts and just before planned break times.

What do you imagine we invariably found? That's right – many, many examples of truly poor service…very often delivered by some of our most trusted people. Sharper TMs very quickly learned how to not find themselves in the embarrassing position of sitting in Monday meetings with their boss and peer group listening to some of their favourite advisers treating customers like fools. Some team members were behaving this way just to get off calls quickly in order to get out for a coffee, pack up and go home or even just to get back to a group conversation about tomorrow's football. Smart TMs understood that they could avoid Monday morning awkwardness by consistently listening to more calls than the standard two calls per agent per week quality monitoring requirement. They discovered individual issues early and addressed them in no uncertain terms by reading the riot act to anyone on shift over the weekend who was likely to be found out when listening to random calls in the Monday morning sessions. They took the direct approach by letting staff know that higher numbers of calls would be monitored over the weekend and anyone found to be dropping quality standards would be subject to further investigation.

I'm not at all fond of the 'stick' approach to changing behaviours but, when used appropriately and sparingly alongside more considered performance management techniques, short-term improvements can be driven.

These sessions also raised questions around Team Manager behaviours on weekend shifts and, disappointingly, it was not uncommon for me to discover that some managers were more laissez-faire than others around general floor behaviours. In fact, I would occasionally find that a manager had let staff go home before the end of their planned shift or even left the building early themselves without informing a line manager or real-time management of their intention. On one occasion, due to noises overheard in the background of calls recorded late on a Friday evening, I discovered that some managers and agents were playing against each other in an almost full scale basketball match on the floor whilst the more conscientious advisers continued to handle calls from customers. The aftermath of that investigation wasn't pretty and at least two management careers ended as a result.

On a more positive note, call recordings are the best coaching tool available to you as a manager and development coach. Being in a position to highlight an individual's areas for improvement using examples of their own work alongside a best practice comparison call is a facility that should never be taken for granted. Side-by-side support and live remote call listening are extremely useful teaching techniques in their own right but the selective use of recorded material can give you all the evidence you'll ever need to aid your efforts to take your team members to the next level of capability. It's therefore crucial that you quickly learn how to access the call recording platform, search for calls you need to support your development sessions and become expert in downloading, editing, packaging and storing the relevant material. You also must be in a position to easily get to what you've stored for use in coaching and training presentations.

My advice to you would be to ask a helpful and capable TM colleague to show you the basics of the application (any good manager should be happy to offer support and advice to a new colleague). Let them take you through how to log in, where to find and play back recordings and how to create easily accessible files for storage purposes. Equally important, ask them about what most commonly goes wrong when using the software. Find out if it locks you out if too many other people are accessing at the same time or if there is a time limit on your session. Enquire also about how best to use the search function and if there are any shortcuts that might save you time and heartache in the future.

Next, speak to the administrator of the system to make sure you have a login generated and full access to all the functions you will require. Get her to take you through a technical overview of how the application works and what you should and should not do during daily use. For example, call recordings may contain secure customer information and, if that's true, for compliance reasons should not be downloaded onto personal folders in the C drive of your PC or laptop nor saved to a portable device of any kind. Also, audio recordings take up a lot of shared drive space and your IT department won't be at all happy with you if the company's shared network drives become clogged up with forgotten downloaded recordings. Again, building good relationships with IT support professionals will pay dividends for you in no time at all.

There are three ubiquitous applications you will use on an everyday basis. You may already know a little about them but I would suggest that you dedicate a little time to becoming really proficient in each. Being even half expert will save you masses of time when you most need it and give you a head start in any comparison with your colleagues' administration skills. To support you in using these three essential programmes please pay close attention to this piece of advice:

Learn To Touch-Type !!

It's easier than you think and there are literally hundreds of cheap programmes and applications that will help make it fun to learn and keep you on the right track. This one skill will speed up all your admin tasks immeasurably and buy you time to do the face-to-face people related work that is at the core of what you should be trying to achieve….it's also great to show off to others. Don't let other TMs or advisers know that you can touch-type then watch their faces as they witness you doing it for the first time!

To get you started as a high-speed typist here are the basics:

1. Place the four fingers of your left hand on the A,S,D and F keys on the middle row of the keyboard. This will always be your left-hand starting position.
2. Place the fingers of your right hand on the J,K,L and ; keys on the middle row of the keyboard. This will always be your right-hand starting position.
3. Place both thumbs on the space bar. This is all that your thumbs will ever be used for.
4. Begin to type very slowly moving your hands up and down rows as you reach for the keys that sit in the top and bottom corners of the standard QWERTY layout. Always return to your starting positions between words.
5. Use your little finger (pinky) to hit the 'shift' keys on both sides and your right pinky to hit 'return'.
6. Divide the keyboard into small groups of letters and numbers then decide which of the fingers of each hand will be responsible for always hitting these keys. You should aim for 4 to 6 keys per finger at the most. Furthest left and right keys should be struck by the little fingers of each hand then change fingers as you move inwards.
7. Begin very, very slowly and make sure you use all your fingers and thumbs for the correct keys.
8. Once you feel sufficiently competent, try looking only at the screen and not at your fingers on the keyboard. When you are able to do this and achieve a high degree of speed and accuracy you will be a fully fledged touch-typist!

Quick word of warning for you – this skill takes a lot of practice to master. It doesn't come naturally to anyone who has for years been battering out documents using only the first fingers of each hand. To begin with your instincts will resist the change and you'll begin to tell yourself that you are hopeless and that the whole thing's not worth the hassle. If you persevere (don't let yourself be put off by minor setbacks) you'll find the battle becomes easier to win and that, incrementally, you will see tiny improvements in speed and accuracy every day.

How many words per minute should you be aiming for? Well, the guys who compete in the speed typing world championships – yes there is such a thing - can hit 180 WPM with almost 100% accuracy. Professionals who do the whole typing thing for a living will sit closer to 100 WPM with 100% accuracy. Beginners should aim for 25 words per minute with 90% accuracy as a starting point then progress to progressive targets of 40/95% then 60/98%.

I genuinely hope you'll take this advice on board as being able to type quickly and accurately may metaphorically save your bacon at some point in the future……and it's a wonderful party trick to impress your friends with.

Anyway, back to the three key applications you will use every day as a Team Manager. As ever, my advice to you is to start your learning early in your career, get ahead of the curve compared to how able your management colleagues appear to be and aim to become the strongest user of each within the operations management team. You've no idea how much respect can be won by being very capable in this area and also how many potential future opportunities will arise simply because you have the lethal combination of the right skills combined with an enthusiastic 'can-do' attitude.

The programmes are Microsoft Outlook®, Microsoft Word® and Microsoft Excel®. All three are registered trademarked components of Microsoft's Office 365® suite.

It's unlikely that you'll receive any formal training in how to use these programmes. To be honest, most people have had personal email accounts for a number of years and will have picked up most of the basic knowledge required to make Outlook work for them without too much help. Word and Excel are slightly trickier and it's very likely that you'll need some support to help you do the more complicated things they're capable of. So, as ever, I suggest that every time you come up against small things you're not sure of how to do simply ask a friendly colleague. Most people are only too happy to help out a newbie and show off their knowledge at the same time. Don't be afraid to approach the people who seem to know how to get things done. Next step is to take what you've learned then practice, practice, practice until you can do it with your eyes shut. After that get onto

YouTube and watch some of the millions of helpful videos that outline how to get the basics right alongside tips and tricks that will take you to the next level of user expertise. Then practice, practice, practice the new things you've just learned until they become second nature.

At some point it will be worth investing a few quid on formal online courses from the likes of Reed.co.uk and janets.org.uk as this will take you through all you'll require to move towards expert user level. You can also elect to sit evaluations and become certificated if that suits your future plans. Much of the content will cost you less than £10 per course and the knowledge you gain can prove to be invaluable.

Outlook will become your single point of daily written communication to your team, colleagues, line manager and the outside world. From here you will send and receive emails, arrange and receive meeting invitations, plan your activities using the calendar function and access the diaries of those with whom you want to arrange face-to-face or group sessions. Needless to say, Outlook can do far more than what I've listed above but it's likely that you won't need it to do much more that what I've suggested.

Jumping off point to becoming an efficient regular user from day one should be learning how to use these very basic functions:

1. Learn how to open an email that has been sent to you.
2. Learn how to open any attached files and store content when required.
3. Practice writing and sending emails using the correct business standard style and etiquette.
4. Start to attach files to emails when appropriate. (Tip: look for the paperclip symbol)
5. Build your Outlook contacts and address list and create regular contact groups. This will save you a great deal of time when sending emails and invitations as you will not have to type in each individual address.
6. Practice using Outlook to send meeting invitations using the Calendar function. Learn how to accept and reject invitations sent to you.
7. Adopt the Calendar as your default work diary using the reminder function to keep you on track on busy days.

8. Learn how to sort your inbox and sent box by sender and recipient so you can easily find priority mail.

It's very likely that you will receive thirty or more emails a day and you will be expected to be across all of them. You will have to create your own system for prioritising each mail. In simple terms you should respond quickly to anything that your line manager has asked you to work on – make those your top priority. At the opposite end of the scale you should read and absorb anything that you have been CC'd into then store for reference only in a low priority folder. Only you can determine how to prioritise your responses as every workplace is different.

To make life easy for yourself I would give top priority to anything from your line manager where an action or reply has been requested. Try to be one of the first to respond without dropping anything else that is important and that you're only halfway through. It's not essential to be the very first to respond to every email from your boss every time so take your time getting a good, relevant, detailed response together and make sure it's sent in time to meet any deadline but do not drop everything else to make it happen unless it's super-urgent.

On the subject of deadlines, please have the guts to let people know when their request is unreasonable. For example, imagine you receive an email from Human Resources asking you to provide them with the original 'right to work' visas for the four foreign nationals in your team by lunchtime of the next day. Don't confirm immediately if that's possible – I would suggest that you check how quickly you can speak to each of the agents concerned and ensure that they are able to supply you with the documents before replying.

You may discover that one or more of the guys concerned is on leave or off sick and cannot be contacted. On the other hand, you may be able to get a hold of all of them but find some of them can't easily lay their hands on the relevant paperwork. You may even be in the position where you will be on rostered time off on the day of the deadline and will not be available to collect the visas and hand them to HR (though you could ask a trusted colleague to do this for you in your absence).

The point I'm making is that there can be any number of legitimate reasons why you may not be able to meet a short notice deadline and you must verify for yourself how viable it is for you to meet the deadline before making rash promises. Don't be afraid to explain to the sender why it may not be possible to hit their timescale as long as you can offer up an alternative, realistic date and time by which you can guarantee to achieve what's required. By all means pull out all the stops to be helpful as supporting your HR colleagues is the decent thing to do – and you can bet your bottom dollar that you'll need them to support you in the future – but don't promise something you cannot deliver. Remember that an email requesting action within a very short deadline may be genuinely business-critical or may just be the sign of someone else's panic due to having left it too late to deliver promises they've made to their managers. Experience will tell you which is which. Do not agree to something that might not be possible for you to achieve as you will end up looking foolish and unreliable.

How To Win Friends and Influence People

Here's a final few paragraphs on the topic of email communication. I've included this as I have spent weeks of my life over the last twenty years dealing with issues caused by the tone of some comms between staff. Frankly, I can now very easily lose my temper with anyone reporting to me who causes upset by email. The reason for my potential loss of control? Simple, we are now in the third decade of the 21st century and I don't believe there is a person on the planet who doesn't know how to be polite and respectful when using electronic communication. Work-related email is not social media. So, when HR come to me with a legitimate complaint about a member of my team who has upset someone elsewhere in the business through impolite language in written comms it's pretty safe to say that the guilty party will be left in no doubt about how I feel about him and what will happen in the event of any repeat performance. Now I know organisations will have differing 'house' styles of communication by email. Some like to be upbeat and begin with a nice 'Hi Mary' or even a 'Hey Jimbo!' while others get straight to the point with just Mary or Jim followed by a short, matter of fact comment or request. Some like to sign off with a 'Cheers Mate' or a plain old 'Regards' or 'Best'. On the other hand a briefer more clipped finish may be all that's expected. I've worked with some people who don't bother with either a salutation or goodbye, just a few words bashed out in a hurry telling the world what they want or giving their opinion in no uncertain terms. Whatever the most commonly used style is within your business then make sure you follow it. Don't turn the spotlight on yourself as the person who is trying to make a point about attempting to change what your colleagues have been doing for years before you turned up.

On the next page I've given you two real-life examples of emails I have received in recent times. Both were received late on a Friday afternoon and had an impact on how I felt about myself and my work as I tried to enjoy the weekend with my family. Read both carefully and think about how you would feel if you received something like this. Then consider how you would react to the senders when you see them on Monday morning.

Example 1:
From: Louise (Planning)
Subject: Bank Holiday Team Manager Staffing

Hi Kenny,

Just a quick note to say thanks for the work your team have done on planning Team Manager cover across the next bank holiday.

There are a couple of small things I still need a little more detail on before I present the finished plan to Resource Planning. Can you please tell me:

1. What level of shrinkage are you building into your planning assumptions? Is it the standard bank holiday 30% that we use for agents or do you think a different number is appropriate as we have lower absence within the TM community?
2. I see you have Alison and Rob on the late shift on the Sunday but Rob mentioned to me in passing that he was planning to take the full weekend as planned leave. Can you confirm?

Sorry for landing this on you late on a Friday but can you get back to me by close of play on Monday of next week?

I appreciate all your help with this and please don't hesitate to call me on my mobile over the weekend if you need more information.

Regards,

Lou

Example 2:
From: Douglas (Project Management)

Subject: Speech Analytics Pilot

Ken – still waiting for the report you promised on this. Not looking for chapter and verse just initial thoughts so really can't get my head around why it's taking you so long. Needless to say you're holding up a business critical initiative and as programme manager I'm responsible for making sure all feedback to the board is delivered on time. I need this for first thing Monday at the latest and if I don't receive it by then I'll have to raise the issue with Dominic (Managing Director). This isn't the first time I've had to chase you for this and I've no intention of doing it again.

Douglas

No prizes for guessing which of these two mails elicited the fastest and most helpful response?

I was so keen to help Louise out that I stayed late in the office on the Friday to catch up with Rob about his plans. I then emailed her the information she was looking for and sent her a text to let her know it was done and wish her a good weekend.

The first thing I did when I received Doug's email was to go onto Amazon Prime to see if I could get a baseball bat delivered before Monday morning in time for the encounter I was planning with Douglas in the company car park. Once I got that mad notion out of my head I checked my sent mail box so that I could be sure of my ground. I knew I had sent the paper he was looking for two days earlier but that he hadn't read it as I had received no 'read receipt'.

My next thought was pretty spiteful in that I considered replying to him to point out his error while copying in our Managing Director and Ruth who was Doug's line manager…..then I thought better of that idea. What would have been the point in being so petty? My relationship with Doug would be ruined and it's likely the MD and Ruth would just be annoyed by the fact two of their senior people were squabbling in this way.

So, I re-sent the original report to Douglas then sent him an abrupt text telling him to look again at his inbox as he'd had the original since Wednesday of the same week. He replied, without apology or thanks, to say his inbox had been full and had eventually found what I'd sent. Still determined to 'punish' him I sent another text saying I was pleased he now had what he needed before the Monday deadline and that I'd catch up with him first thing Monday morning to have a chat about the email he had sent me earlier. I knew that would spark a response from him but I ignored his call on Saturday morning and a text following that in which he asked me what I wanted to see him about. I wanted him to stew.

I spent the whole weekend in a seriously bad mood planning what I was going to say to him come Monday – this is where it gets ridiculous – alongside what I would do if it turned into a physical fight. I didn't get to see him till late on Monday afternoon and when I did it turned out to be something of an anti-climax. We went into a meeting room and he asked why I wanted to speak to him. I had planned the speech while lying awake on the Sunday night so I told him I didn't appreciate the tone of his email on Friday and that he should have checked the facts before sending anything like that to me. I let him know that I especially didn't like his threat of escalation to the MD and his final comment about constantly having to 'chase' me for late submissions. Then – as I often do – I softened my approach. I told him that I thought he was one of the 'good guys' and that we all understood the pressures of delivering a complex project on time. I hoped that, in future, when a situation like this arises in future he would simply pop round to my desk and ask if I'd had time to get the promised report done. That would give me the opportunity to reassure him about where I was up to with it and guarantee when I'd get it over to him. He offered an apology of sorts and agreed he'd panicked a little as he was to deliver his presentation on Monday but some of the information he needed was still outstanding – including, he wrongly believed – my report.

Can you see how much unnecessary upset and angst was caused by one ill thought out email sent late on a Friday? Any issues could have been resolved quickly and easily in a five-minute chat in the office and two families wouldn't have had their weekends spoiled by a pair of silly, grumpy and frankly rather childish dads.

My point in all of this is pretty straight forward:

Intelligent and mature use of MS Outlook will help you build an organised and professional approach to your work. Mis-use will single you out as a rank amateur who is not really sure of his next move. If I were beginning a career in management I would certainly try to develop a respectful, considerate, business-like style of email communication. My advice to you is this – do not deliberately set out to criticise, threaten or antagonise colleagues or clients. Try to make each email request feel like a joint attempt to take things forward in a positive way. A considerate and collaborative style will, I promise, bring better and faster results and your working life will be all the easier for it.

Once you've become a competent user of Outlook then it's time to get to grips with Microsoft Excel and Word. These applications allow you to clearly and professionally present and share business-related data and information. Let's look first at Excel.

As a Team Manager you will, from time to time, be asked to present information relating to your team in an organised, easy to understand universal format. Other departments will expect to be able to manipulate your data without having to convert it into something more user friendly. The medium you will utilise will most likely be MS Excel.

At its most basic this programme allows you to produce spreadsheets for storing, sorting and communicating information relating to your team. As you become more expert you will be in a position to produce complicated graphs and charts, introduce formulae that will automatically update and share your data quickly with the whole of your business and allow you to perform complex and large calculations as well as extensive data analysis. It's also great to be able to create the kind of 'dashboard' for each team member and your team as a whole that can support 121s and performance management appraisals.

Can I suggest that you get started now and in a very small way. Try to take tiny, incremental daily steps forward and don't attempt to move on until you've mastered the very basic functions I'm going to list here. Plan to complete each step in one day and spend one final day simply practising what you've learned using real-world data from your team or numbers you can simply make up for yourself. Again, YouTube should be your 'go to' spot on the internet where you'll find literally hundreds of videos covering how to do this really basic stuff. Don't get carried away and jump ahead to more complex tasks – just get your head around the easy things first.

So, here are the basic Excel functions you should become expert at performing – I've given you a picture of what the finished simple spreadsheet should look like when complete:

Contact Centre Team Management

1. Open the programme and select a new blank workbook to make a start on. Name and save the workbook in an accessible folder.
2. Learn what cells and columns are then select four columns and put a heading for each of them in the cell at the top: Name, Login, Calls and Sales respectively. Save and Close.
3. Learn what a row is then select four rows under your column heading 'Name' and insert one of the following in a cell each row: Ann, James, Steve and Total. Save and Close.
4. In the 'Login' column select the appropriate cell and enter: Ann1, James1 and Steve1. Then select 'Calls' and enter 20, 17 and 24 respectively followed by the numbers followed by 2, 0 and 1 under 'Sales'. Learn how to name the worksheet on the tab at the bottom of the screen by right clicking on the sheet tab, click 'Rename' and type the words 'Sales Project' then Save.
5. Learn how to produce a total of calls and sales by left clicking and highlighting the cells in each column. Look to the bar at the bottom of the screen and you'll see the word 'Sum' with the total of the numbers in the cells you've highlighted (you can also use the AutoSum feature on the Home tab at the top left of your screen). Save total calls and sales in cells in the fourth row under the relevant columns.
6. Spend a day practising what you've learned. Create larger spreadsheets with more columns, rows and more extensive data. Study how to copy and paste your tables to Outlook, Word and other Excel worksheets.
7. Spend a little time messing around and experimenting with the vast array of functions you'll find in the Home tab. Learn how to format your tables using a variety of borders, colours and fonts then look at how things like AutoSum automatically enters a formula for you and think about how you could use this feature going forward.

Name	Login	Calls	Sales
Ann	Ann1	20	2
James	James1	17	0
Steve	Steve1	24	1
Total		61	3

Now I know this is really simple stuff and that many of you will already be able to complete much more complicated tasks but that's not really the point of this exercise. I want all of you to be able to master the basics very early in your careers and be able to produce simple tables at the drop of a hat because that's most of what will be expected of you in this regard as a Team Manager. The guys in your Reporting and Resource Planning teams will require expert standard Excel skills to perform their roles properly but you won't. Sure it's great to be able to produce your own complex RAG pivot tables (spreadsheets that allow you to easily sort data by a number of different KPIs then split into red, amber and green performance standards to allow you to quickly identify the members of your team who are struggling) and 3D infographics but, unless you're planning to move away from Operations into one of the support departments, you don't actually need these skills to be a great TM….in fact that stuff can simply prove to be a distraction from the real work that requires to be done with your group. Focus on what matters in improving the performance of each of the members of your team. The things you that will make you a great manager and leader won't happen when sitting behind a PC. Fancy charts and graphics are great to look at but it's the side-by-side, people related stuff that makes the difference in the end.

Let's look now at MS Word. This package will become your default medium for producing documents and reports and will often incorporate charts, tables, photographs and artwork. For example, you may want to produce a monthly newsletter or briefing for your team to be distributed on paper or electronically via your company's intranet. More importantly you will often be expected to type up notes of return to work interviews, disciplinary meetings, monthly 121s and annual reviews. It's, therefore, massively important that you become a competent user as early in your career as a manager as possible.

To get started we will practice a few very simple steps which you should work on until you can perform each automatically without really having to think about them. Once you're able to this it will be time to get on to YouTube again and learn how to complete some more complicated tasks – bearing in mind my earlier advice that your team members are best served by having you work with them side-by-side rather that constantly sitting behind your PC designing new spreadsheets, forms and briefings.

Anyway, follow these simple instructions and see how you get on. If you are already a competent MS Word user then teach yourself two more complex functions like converting a list to a table or adding placeholder text.

1. Open Word and select a blank document to begin working on. Make sure you have selected the 'Home' tab on the light blue bar at the top of the page then find the sub-section titled 'Styles'. Click on 'No Spacing' as this will mean you can type normally without double spacing between lines.
2. Type the words 'Monthly Newsletter' at the top in bold by first clicking on the bold capital letter 'B' in the Font section of the same bar at the top of your screen. Select the words you've just typed by holding down the left button on your mouse and dragging the mouse across. Centre the title by selecting the appropriate icon in the 'Paragraph' component on the bar at the top of your screen. Save the document as 'Newsletter' then close.
3. Open Microsoft Word and select your document. Once open, move the cursor down four lines from your title then type a paragraph of 50 random words. Format this to appear the way you want it by selecting the appropriate alignment icon in the 'Paragraph' section on the bar at the top of your page. Always copy the in-house format style used within your organisation – don't go rogue and decide to invent your own as you'll soon be asked to fall in line with everyone else.
4. Now you'll learn how to add a picture, table or artwork to your document. So, move the cursor down two lines from your typed paragraph then click on 'Insert' on the bar at the top left of your screen. You will see that you can choose from a number of options including tables, pictures, charts, screenshots etc.
5. Select 'Table'. A 10 x 8 grid will appear. Just like Excel the squares represent cells arranged in columns and rows. Using your mouse run the arrow over the grid lighting up four rows in four columns then left click. The table will magically appear at the point in your document where you left off. Using the simple data I gave you in the Excel exercise fill in some of the cells in your new Word table. You can re-size the table, cells, rows or columns by dragging the little crosses you'll find at the corners of your insert.
6. Delete the table and practice inserting shapes, pictures etc. until you're happy that you are competent at using this function.

Microsoft 365 Office™ applications are capable of a myriad of wonderful things and it's all too easy to distract yourself for hours on end creating new sophisticated spreadsheets, charts, forms and documents. I urge you not to attempt to convince yourself that doing this adds value to the work of your team – it doesn't. These are tools to support you in driving the best from and for your people and nothing more. Become highly competent using the basic functions of each application then focus on the things that really matter to your team and the business you work for.

Team Meetings

As a new TM you'll be expected to organise, lead and facilitate effective and worthwhile weekly team meetings. This can be quite challenging if you've never had to do it before. My advice again is to work hard on getting it right the first time then make small, incremental improvements from thereon in. Preparation is everything.

You'll soon be sick of hearing me say this but the best place to start is to sit in on meetings being led by experienced managers you respect and know to be very capable. Don't be afraid to approach a colleague and let them know that this is all new to you and you'd like to get off to a great start. Tell them that sitting in on one of their weekly team sessions would give you pointers on how to organise the agenda, deal with both awkward and helpful input from attendees and ensure that everyone gets something out of the gathering. I can't imagine that any worthwhile colleague would reject such a request and most will be only too willing to help you out.

Once you've been to a couple of good sessions run by other managers you should begin to build a picture in your mind of what the perfect meeting will look like. Here's a list of first steps you should be thinking about:

1. Where will the meeting be held and how will you format the seating? Make sure you book a meeting room where you won't be disturbed and that is large enough for all attendees to get a space round a table that they can lean of for taking notes. Learn how to use the room booking system. Is it electronic or do you simply shove your name up on a form on the door of the room?
2. Send out invites to all attendees using Outlook if possible. Choose a meeting date and time when you know the majority of your team will be on shift. Check for clashes with lunches and breaks, planned training or visits from Prince Charles, your local MP, Gazza or other so called 'dignitaries' (you'd be surprised who some

companies bring along to stare at a couple of hundred people taking phone calls).

3. Prepare and share an agenda well in advance. It has to be concise and cover all subjects you feel must be discussed in the current week. Leave lots of space for feedback from the people in the room. I guarantee they'll have strong opinions on most things and a few will want to string the whole thing out as long as possible to avoid having to go back out to the floor to take calls.

4. Consider appropriate responses to points that may potentially be raised by the team based on what's on your agenda. What is likely to be controversial? If you don't know the correct response to any point raised then tell the group you will find out and get back to them. Do not make something up in an attempt to look knowledgeable and in control – this is a potentially fatal error that can land you in seriously hot water if what you've said isn't consistent with senior management views or misleads and confuses your team members and the other staff they will undoubtably talk to.

5. Take minutes and actions. Minutes are brief notes recording what was discussed at the meeting and who said what. Actions are tasks that have been assigned to one or more members of the attendees with a view to them reporting back when they've completed the task. Keep a record of all actions on your brand new, much envied 'Action Tracker' that you will have just designed using your recently developed Microsoft Word™ skills. Actions and minutes relating to the previous week's meeting should always be your first agenda point.

6. Take firm but polite control of the meeting. It's your job to ensure that it doesn't overrun timewise or spiral out of control when a couple of passionate attendees won't let a particular point rest. You must learn to cover off all planned agenda items without giving disproportionate time to any sticking points. Leave five minutes free at the end of the meeting for a short summary of what may have been discussed.

7. Maintain your sense of humour. Meetings should be informative and fun. Lose the fun and your team will start to dread these sessions. Advisers should look forward to the group getting together once a week as an opportunity to bond and share thoughts on what's important to them. They will want their voices to be heard and it's your job to make them feel that they've each made a valuable contribution. However, don't get carried away with

your role as chief funster. Singling someone out for sarcasm or jokes about their personal appearance or performance at work can lead to all sorts of complaints and grievances being raised. Similarly, gossip or criticism of colleagues in other teams will inevitably get back to them and you can end up in really awkward circumstances if you let your big mouth get the better of you. Take care!!
8. Don't share sensitive information unless you have permission from your line manager to do so. It's inevitable that some individuals will twist what you say at team meetings for their own benefit so you really must not make any potentially controversial statement about company plans or policy unless it's definitely in the public domain. Should there be talk of rumours about company growth or downsizing or a possible change of location your job is to calmly and professionally let the team know that you are not aware of any such plans and, if that should change, they will be the first to know. Do not try to buy respect from your team by sharing business sensitive information in an 'I really shouldn't be telling you this but....' type scenario.

In summary, your weekly team meetings should be educational, informative and entertaining. They should be mini events that all staff look forward to as an opportunity to speak their minds and to learn from their teammates. Sessions must start and finish on time and not impinge on the work that everyone else on the call floor is trying to do while you and your guys are getting together. Clearance from your real-time management team should be obtained before pulling 12 advisers from calls for an hour – be prepared to be interrupted if call volumes suddenly spike as handling customer queries and achieving contractual service levels will trump staff meetings every time. After all, you can pick up again as a group or at 121s when things on the floor are a little quieter.

Due to planned leave, sickness absence and rota'd (my spelling of an often used contact centre term) days off you will not have all of your team available to meet on any given day. It's crucial that you take a little time following up with those who weren't present on the day. This prevents the potential curse of mixed messages and rumours developing.

Store all agendas, minutes and action logs in a file on either your C drive or the company shared drive for easy access. Keep your documents together as a complete set – do not miss any week or any individual record.

Incomplete records demonstrate laziness and sloppiness. If you're going to be professional then make sure you're doing the right things right all the time and not just when you feel like it. It's hard work becoming a strong Team Manager and at times you'll want to take shortcuts and cut corners. I wouldn't if I were you – I've tried it and it leaves you feeling exposed and vaguely uncomfortable. Doing all things 'properly' has its own rewards. It's also the best way to ensure that your team members and the business you work for are getting full value from your efforts.

Find out if your business has a preferred agenda template and use it if they do. If not, go onto Google and find one that best suits your purpose. Keep the tone upbeat and avoid too many messages beginning with the words 'You must not'. Being told as a group where not to park your car, vape, queue for coffee, leave coats and bags etc. is a pain and will totally kill the collective vibe. You'll then find it really difficult to build the more positive atmosphere essential to make the remainder of the session worthwhile. What I tend to do is introduce these kinds of things briefly at the very end with a 'Just one last thing before we go' approach. This is what I would say to the team – try something that vaguely approaches lame humour but gets the message home:

'Listen, I know this won't apply to most of you but it's worth covering off for the new guys and those who haven't heard. Please do me a favour and don't leave your car in the visitor spaces at the front of the building. They're usually booked out for clients and there's loads of space in the main car park for our motors. Remember as well that vaping is only allowed in the shelter at the left of the building as you come through the main gate. While I'm at it please remember for security reasons leave all coats and bags in your locker and not under your desk. If anyone is having difficulty with their locker then let me know and I'll get it sorted. And remember, if you decide to ignore any of this stuff it won't be just me who'll be having a word – you'll be dealing with mad Derek and psycho Irene in Security and they don't take any prisoners. I have it on good authority that they once caught a new trainee queuing at the wrong side of the coffee machine and the wee guy was never seen again. Some say he might have ended up under the new smoking shelter at the back of the building………don't let that be you.'

I wouldn't expect them to be rolling about in the aisles with laughter but it's a simple method of making a serious point within meetings in a way that doesn't bring the group down. Find your own (i.e. funnier) way of doing the same thing without attempting to embarrass or humiliate anyone in particular. If the message doesn't sink in then it's time to take the individuals aside who haven't been paying attention to remind them of the point you tried to make humorously. Ask them why they ignored what you've asked them to think about – it could be they'll have a really good reason or simply made a mistake – then get them to commit to toeing the line from there on in. If, after that, they go on to defy the instruction again then it's clear they are attempting to make a point of some kind or another and you'll have to address it much more directly. In short you have an attitude problem to deal with and you will have to work hard to change that if you also want behaviours to improve. It's likely you'll discover the underlying reason for the belligerence stems from something that has nothing to do with car parking or coffee machines and you will have to address the root issue if you're going to halt the on-going defiance.

Handled badly, situations like these can result in unnecessary and time-consuming disciplinary actions or - even worse – the agent deciding simply to walk out and not return. The kind of '**** you!' gesture aimed at highlighting a lack of empathy and understanding on the part of management. Do everything you reasonably can to prevent this from happening while accepting that some people look to exploit this kind of scenario for their own ends and can do a lot of damage to the morale of the group if not dealt with swiftly but compassionately. Occasionally, letting a genuinely bad apple go can be the best course of action.

To sum up then; plan team meetings carefully, start and finish on time covering all points on the published agenda, keep minutes and an action log to share with those unable to attend and make sure everyone leaves the session feeling better and more positive than when they went in. If you can achieve this at 90% of your group get-togethers then you can consider yourself highly competent. How you handle the other 10% of controversial, PR disasters will determine whether you're becoming a pro or not.

Floor Support

If there's one thing that determines how much respect your team members will have for you it's this. In simple terms, when they are dealing with a seriously difficult customer or contact situation your agents need to know that you have their backs. So, when they shove up their hands looking for help, advice or for you to take over a call as an escalation, they want to be able to do it without feeling they are in some way inconveniencing you. As an empathetic, professional manager you should be happy to get to a raised hand quickly to support your staff member but also to give the customer the best service available.

Now I know what you're thinking (we've all been through it). You're thinking along the lines that you are incredibly busy supporting your boss, the business and other team members and you don't have time to constantly nurse the same people through the day covering off a bunch of stuff you've already taken them through earlier in the week. Wasn't last week's live learning session all about how to make immediate refunds to the card the initial payment came from? If so then why is Mags asking you about it again? Haven't you already told Jason three times how to deal with callers who insist on speaking to a manager? Of course you have – but that's not the point.

Everyone learns at a different pace. Some need constant reassurance while others are very sure of themselves, want to be independent and make their own decisions without asking for support. Others can appear totally confident but in fact are just making it all up as they go along causing untold damage to customers and businesses alike. Some get scared and drop difficult calls half-way through or make totally unnecessary inter-department transfers just to move the customer on to someone else. At any given time all of these things could be going on within your team and if you don't make yourself available for real-time on the floor support you will make the bad stuff much more likely to happen. By being accessible you prevent the kind of panic that leads to poor decision making and dreadful customer service.

I'm not saying that the same old faces should be allowed to pass the buck to you at will forever, nor should you tolerate the same questions being asked of you time and time again. However, it's your responsibility to deliver the kind of coaching that closes these issues off early in an adviser's career. Take time to identify the aspects of the role they most struggle with and focus on getting them to a place where they will only rarely require you to stand beside them while they handle a straightforward customer query. Practice the script they should refer to when a customer demands to speak to a manager. Rehearse that situation a hundred times over until both the agent and you are happy that they can deal with that set of circumstances when they next present themselves. Don't make them feel awkward should they fail as this will discourage them from asking for support next time around.

As I write this I can hear the voices of hundreds of Team Managers I've worked with exclaiming how unrealistic my view is and that my perspective is typical of contact centre senior management who don't actually have to do the work on the ground. Over the years I've thought long and hard about this and I am still convinced that the TM who takes the time to be available for the persistent hand-raisers is in a win/win situation. First, she quickly builds the respect and affection of her team and second, assuming consistent delivery of first class coaching, her team members become self-sufficient earlier in their careers and are less likely to make major errors or be the subject of complaints. Achieving early agent competency through intelligent, patient floor support pays dividends in the long-run as fewer and fewer hands are raised allowing the manager to spend more time on her other priorities.

There is also a clear correlation between early competence and low rates of agent attrition. In short, an agent who is well supported and becomes confident and competent within their initial 12 weeks in the role is much more likely to remain with the company. This means that the experience pool isn't being diluted through the constant turnover of staff while the business saves £2k-£3k that would have to be spent on recruiting and training a new member of staff. There is also evidence that well supported agents have better attendance records on average when compared to those who are left to their own devices or are on the receiving end of the kind of grumpy, reluctant rubbish some managers are guilty of. Think about it – if you were doing your best in a low paid agent role how happy would you be to be met with little or no support on the occasions you most felt vulnerable? How engaged and enthusiastic would you feel? Not at all would be my guess and if it were me in that situation I'd be planning my escape at the earliest opportunity.

Of course, supporting the floor, or 'management by walking about' as it is sometimes known, is about so much more than just responding to cries for help. The opportunities to deliver a thumbs-up or pat on the back are endless. My rule on this is pretty simple - deliver a quick nod or wink or whatever works for you in the direction of anyone you hear doing something well. A brave attempt at an upsell or a super polite and efficient call summary and ending should be met with mini celebrations. Positive recognition is important to everyone in the workplace and the low level, every day thumbs-up costs nothing but lets your guys know that you appreciate all the great stuff they're doing. This is especially true when calls are queuing in their hundreds and everyone is under pressure. An inquisitive look or a gentle 'keep it calm' wave of the hand in the direction of an adviser with steam beginning to shoot from his ears can also be helpful in letting him know that you're there if he needs you but also that you don't want a difficult call to become impossible through rising tempers. Follow this up with a smile and nod as you sense him controlling the situation more effectively and you may just have prevented a costly complaint.

New staff will obviously require more support than your established people. Rather than perceive this as a time-consuming nuisance try to spot the opportunities to promote strong relationships and develop established agents who are keen to build the skills and experience required for them to move into training or junior management roles.

The soft landing that grad bays are designed to provide for new trainees going live should see them ease into the call floor environment in a way that builds confidence without the horror of having to deal with challenging customers alone. The step after this can be a challenge however. Suddenly they will be amongst strangers and there's all sorts of talk of targets and managing call handling time. For many it is at this point that the reality of what's expected of them starts to kick in. Your job must be to make this transition as pain free as possible. This is achieved by absorbing them into your group from day one. Make them feel like an equal partner and not an excluded newbie who has to fight to be heard. Help them get to know every other member of the team. Remember, if a new member of staff can make at least one close connection amongst the existing community in the first few weeks of their tenure then that person is much more likely to persevere when things get tough for them. For you this will result in a faster route to competence, better attendance and lower staff turnover.

In every team there will be a small number of 'try-hards' just desperate to get themselves noticed and involved in other things. I love these guys as they have made my life so much easier than it could have been. They are also the people most likely to satisfy your business's on-going need to fill the support and operations roles that consistently become available when new projects are established. The best of them will become your right-hand women and men and will get you out of a hole more often that you can possibly imagine. The very best of them will be running your company in ten years. They are to be encouraged and appreciated and given every opportunity to shine. Your part in their advancement and career progression may well be the thing you become proudest of as you mature into a contact centre professional and away from the over ambitious, self-centred egomaniac you began your working life as. Learn to treasure them.

My point here is simple. Identify a few people you can trust to do the job right and allow them to support the floor at times when you are otherwise occupied and the real-time management team has agreed that there is suitable availability. Each must have the correct level of knowledge and the nurturing personality needed to be effective when supporting a panicking new kid. When you're as certain as you can be that you have selected the best people for the role then it's time to sit down with them and establish some ground rules. Give them a very small number of very simple instructions and keep an eye on them. Hold regular debriefings to listen to what they have to say then agree next steps. Thank them and make them feel appreciated.

When putting together a small group of right-hand, supporting agents please take time to create a fair and transparent selection process. Managers can badly damage team morale by simply tapping their favourite people on the shoulder whenever they need help. This kind of thing feeds the belief amongst your team members that they can only make progress in their ambitions if they somehow break into your inner circle of favoured colleagues. Nothing fractures a happy group faster than obvious favouritism and flagrant disregard for the people you happen not to go to lunch with every day or drink in the pub with on a Friday at 6pm.

Most members of your team will harbour work related aspirations of some kind and it's important that you understand and nurture these from the beginning of your time together. Once armed with this information you must work hard to find ways of feeding their aspirations while supporting the needs of your business. Doing this well brings a whole bunch of benefits for all concerned. By now you should be able to guess what they are: higher levels of engagement leading to lower absence and staff turnover, strong team morale and appropriate skills development leading to better succession planning and so on. All massively important things to achieve if you want to be a success in your role.

So, how do you get this aspect of the job right? It's pretty simple actually and it's mainly about consistency of messaging and communication.

First, let all team members know that you are looking for volunteers to support new staff on the floor. Describe how much knowledge and experience you believe will be required to fulfil the brief effectively and take time to outline the characteristics of a good floor support coach (patience, empathy, enthusiasm). Ask all interested parties to make themselves known to you by close of play on Friday of the week you are in – or earlier if you have an urgent requirement. Ensure that all of your team members have received the same message on what you're looking for. If anyone is off sick or on planned leave then put something in your diary to remind you to talk to them on their return.

Next, have a ten-minute private conversation with all who express an interest. If you don't believe that a volunteer has sufficient product or system knowledge or you're worried about their ability to keep a lid on their frustration when simple concepts aren't grasped first time then it's crucial that you give them the necessary feedback. Alongside this you must offer them a roadmap to help them achieve the levels of technical and emotional competency required for them to be considered for future support roles. Never close down an individual's aspirations at this point by telling them that they're 'just not suited' for a particular function. This leads to disaffection and disengagement that can easily be avoided by presenting an individual with achievable challenges which, when met, result in the kind of rewards that demonstrate progress towards the competency required to become a trusted floor support coach. Palpable failure to hit the mark can also in some ways be useful in that it forces the insightful aspiring adviser to reconsider their suitability for support or management roles. This form of soul-searching often results in a positive change of direction or a redoubled determination to develop the skills necessary to achieve the original objective.

Treat every expression of willingness to help out as an opportunity to support, motivate and engage your people. From this group will come your future leaders. Harness this enthusiasm and use it as fuel to drive forward your efforts to build a successful and cohesive team. Handle all volunteers with respect and reward them with a well-lit way ahead. Remember that many people will find it difficult to put themselves forward. They may not want to be perceived as being pushy or conceited and will have a tendency to hold back waiting to be asked rather than gamble on the potential humiliation of being rejected.

Consider why some of your best people may not have put themselves forward. Is it that they simply need a little more encouragement or is there more to it than that? Could it be that they feel in some way aggrieved about something and are using this exercise to draw attention to their resentment? It's your job to spot this possibility and attempt to get to the bottom of what the issue may be then take steps to resolve it if it's in your power to do so.

Maintain an open mind in respect of who you believe may or may not be suitable to support your less experienced people. Try not to jump to instant negative judgements. It's lazy to perceive an individual in one-dimensional terms. Be truthful at this point – do you quickly dismiss some people as too old, too young, too inappropriate, too silly, too careless, too lazy, too smelly? Let me answer this for you – yes you do and I know this because we're all guilty of it to some extent. From time to time you will have to let go of these preconceptions. I'm not advocating rewarding persistent poor behaviours but it's important to realise that occasionally offering low-level responsibilities to previously seemingly irresponsible people can deliver surprisingly good results. On more than one occasion I've been amazed to witness the apparent transformation from team joker to star coach of the guy many casual observers would just have written off as a bit of an irritant. It takes honest feedback, clear messaging and close supervision to pull this off but it's worth it when it works. Don't write off the guy who comes to you and says "Listen boss, I know I've been a bit daft in the past and that we haven't always got on but I'd like to put myself forward for a support role".

Clearly you won't always be in a position to present an immediate opportunity for redemption but you can jointly create a roadmap to potential success. This will give you time to observe how serious the agent is in their intentions and it will offer a clearer view of how capable he is of hitting agreed behavioural milestones along the way. It's really satisfying when these situations work out well but, in my experience, sadly too many end in failure. It may be that your company HR policies, customs or practices won't permit anyone with a poor disciplinary record to put themselves forward for even an informal role change (best to find this out in advance of any agreement) or that the individual reverts to type and goes AWOL or generates a customer complaint that is investigated and upheld. No matter what the reason I estimate that 75% of your well intentioned attempts to rehabilitate through adding personal responsibility may not succeed and you will then have to deal with what is likely to be a tricky set of circumstances. This it is why it's critical to discuss the doomsday scenario with the adviser ahead of agreeing the roadmap i.e. "How will you feel and behave if this initiative doesn't succeed?".

I can guarantee the response will be something resembling a pledge to "feel disappointed but learn from the experience then work harder to make sure the next attempt at a support role will be successful". In reality you are much more likely to see toys being thrown from the pram followed by deliberate attempts to undermine both you as their manager and the new people you have selected to help you with floor support. The rejected adviser will most probably brief against you with other staff. Both their attendance and attitude to the work and workplace may suffer and you will have to work really hard to keep them on-side. Of course you should remind them of the pledge they made to get keep their head down and work harder but don't expect that to have too much of an impact on future behaviours.

Humiliation

The essence of this – and why I'm spending so much time writing about this – is that the agent in this scenario may feel humiliated. Humiliation of your staff (deliberately or by accident) is a folly to be avoided at all costs. Please learn this now; no-one ever forgives the manager who has publicly humiliated him in the workplace. The incident will never be forgotten and the aggrieved party will hold it against you until their dying day. You will never get him fully on-side again and his view of you may impact your future career opportunities should he feel strongly enough to communicate his feelings about you to decision makers within your organisation who are prepared to listen.

Apart from anything else, humiliation hurts. Why would you want anyone to feel bad about themselves? If that kind of thing gives you a buzz then I suggest you go and look for a job more suited to your talents and characteristics. Take it from me, you're not a fit person to manage people.

So, how do you avoid humiliating someone in the workplace? Actually, it's pretty simple. Do not in any way be publicly critical of an individual. Totally avoid public comments about how someone dresses, speaks, walks, eats, smells, stands or where they live or who they are married to or their religious beliefs, political views or their sexuality or the car they drive.....anything at all in fact that is very personal to that individual and that they may be sensitive about. I know there will be times where you feel a little light-hearted 'banter' may help boost the mood of a group but you could easily misjudge what is appropriate and what is not. Needless to say, this list must also include the quality of a team member's work and their career aspirations which is why your rejection of them after they have unsuccessfully applied for a support role may be perceived by them as a very public humiliation administered by you. Needless to say they will not understand their failure to secure the role as their fault – you, as the decision maker, will be public enemy number one.

All legitimate workplace related critical remarks must be made in private as part of a planned feedback session. It is wholly appropriate for a manager to discuss company dress code, eating at desks, personal hygiene, expressions of political or religious dogma etc. with a team member if the TM believes that any of these is becoming an issue that is affecting team performance or culture.

Don't make the same people repeatedly the butt of your 'humour' at team meetings. You shouldn't be surprised to learn that an agent may smile at a joke aimed at them on one day then raise a grievance against you the next time you attempt something similar. What's amusing to someone on Monday may feel hurtful on Wednesday of the same week. You cannot know what is happening in an individual's life at any point so a cutting remark made in public may be all it takes for them to decide that enough is enough and a complaint to HR is duly made.

I can't tell you the amount of times I've investigated complaints against a TM or Ops Manager where this kind of situation arises. Often an agent being formally investigated for an unrelated breach of an organisation's code of conduct will make a counter claim of bullying or humiliation against the manager who started the initial investigation. This is a common tactic designed to distract from why the disciplinary action is happening in the first place. These attempts to muddy the water usually fail but can leave behind awkward scenarios that have to be dealt with before everyone returns to their usual roles and relationships. An agent lashing out at their manager in this way can easily cast doubt about the manager's overall capability and his (it does tend to be a male manager in my experience) emotional intelligence. Picking on a member of staff to amuse your team is insensitive and will lose you friends and the respect of your peers in the long run.

So my advice to you is this – don't aim your barbed attempts at humour at any individual. This applies to your own team members and any other colleagues. I can guarantee your supposedly funny remarks will get back to the subjects and you may find yourself on the end of some very awkward conversations if they confront you with their concerns. This is the kind of thing that ends up in drunken altercations in the pub after work on a Friday followed by shamed faces on return to the office on Monday morning…..followed thereafter by someone like me dragging you into a meeting room in an effort to find out what happened before deciding what kind of disciplinary action will result (this is a good time for you to go away and look up the meaning of the term 'vicarious liability'!).

Try not to publicly criticise, humiliate or poke fun at any one person in your workplace. Save your jokes for things like yourself (a little bit of mild self-deprication can be very endearing), the food in the cafeteria, the traffic on the way to the office etc. It's a good thing to demonstrate you have a sense of humour….just choose your targets very carefully.

Robbie – A Case in Point

What follows is a true account of a real-life situation which I was involved in a number of years ago. I make no apologies for the length of the tale or the amount of detail I've included. I'd really like you to take the time to consider how you may find yourself in a similar scenario and to critique the actions of me and my group of Team Managers.

If you take nothing else from what follows please remember this – good management is very often about dealing well with a number of conflicting demands and last-minute crises at the same time. Bad things rarely happen in isolation. Be prepared to act on a number of fronts simultaneously and handle each as well as you can without tying yourself up in knots attempting to achieve the 'perfect' solution.

To an outsider Robbie would have looked like a model agent. He knew more about our products and customer management system than just about anyone in the building. He was pleasant, helpful, supportive and fun to be around. Most of the agent community liked and respected him while some of the Team Manager group avoided him because he made them feel inadequate. They often had to defer to Robbie when a complex system related problem arose and many advisers would simply ask him for help with a challenging issue rather than approach a TM because they believed they would get better quality info. He was also often called upon to showcase our capability at agent level when prospective new clients would join us for a walk round. This got up the noses of one or two managers who, rather than take time to improve their own system knowledge, would gripe about Robbie and how it seemed he could do what he liked on the call floor.

Robbie did have one major flaw, however - he was easily bored. Robbie is still possibly the most easily distracted man I've ever met. In addition, his disciplinary record was really poor due to persistent absence. When he was bored Robbie simply wouldn't bother coming to work. When he did come to work – and was allowed a little bit of freedom to informally support other members of staff – he was a star.

Everyone was keen to get Robbie to a place where he could utilise his skills and personality for the benefit of our centre. We agreed this had to be done formally and in a disciplined role that would be overseen by the most suitable Team Manager.

As ever, we were looking for a few good, trustworthy advisers to become floor support people looking after our most recent intake of staff. In addition we would educate them in some basic functions of the TM role and give them the opportunity to operate as team 'captains' when their own line managers had to be elsewhere. Robbie's manager came to me to ask me to consider Robbie for the team captain position on her team. She made a really great case around harnessing his talents for the benefit of the business and that agents liked and respected him. She firmly believed that the time was now right to give Robbie a little bit of responsibility and that this could be the making of him. I wasn't so sure but agreed to think about her proposal as long as she sent me a paper outlining how she would go about educating Robbie and guaranteeing that he wouldn't once more simply go off the rails when the repetitive nature of the work became too dull for him. I also asked for a copy of his disciplinary record to ensure that we would not be contradicting company policy and rules around who could and could not be considered for seconded positions like this.

Robbie had no current or live 'offences' on his disciplinary record so we were able to consider him for a seconded role. In addition, his TM put together an amazing paper covering the jobs Robbie would be tasked with, how we would measure his success and how she would support and manage him throughout the proposed three-month period. I spoke to him as well and he convinced me that this was the kind of opportunity he had been waiting for and promised me that he wouldn't become distracted and disappear for days or take his eyes off the ball in terms of what was expected him.

For four weeks Robbie was the star of our show. He truly excelled himself and his commitment to the tasks we set was inspirational. He even managed to convince the doubters within the TM community that he was the right man for that kind of role.

Every now and again, as a manager, you will have a day when a bunch of things go wrong at the same time then these issues become compounded by a totally unexpected left-field scenario that takes almost everyone by surprise. On these days you do what you can to manage each of the issues in turn and this can sometimes mean putting measures in place that you usually would not countenance. Friday 12th May was one such day.

We had forecast higher than usual inbound call volumes as a price increase had just been notified to two million customers via their monthly bills which had been sent out and posted on-line at the beginning of the week. To counter this expected spike we offered out overtime, agreed shortened lunches and moved shift start points around. Seconded advisers returned to call handling and temporary IVR messaging and script changes were agreed with our client to shorten calls and support us in handling the 25% increase in calls we anticipated. It was going to be tight but we believed we had everything in place to ensure we could still hit our SLA target for the day of 80/30 (80% of all calls offered to be answered within 30 seconds). Every member of staff understood how unusual the situation was and were fully behind the push to get through the day successfully.

Earlier that same week we noticed a sharp increase in sickness absence due to a stomach bug that seemed to be going around. By Friday 12th the bug had ripped through the centre and our absence numbers were double what we would normally expect them to be. Suddenly, almost 20% of staff weren't available for work and we didn't have enough managers to cover the floor across all shifts. Getting through the busiest day of the year and hitting a decent level of service seemed like an almost impossible challenge......and we still had the weekend to worry about (weekend absence and lateness numbers are often higher than what you get Monday to Friday).

As a management team we agreed to each work 12 hour shifts and move our start times to earlier in the day when we expected to be at our busiest. This left us a little light for TM cover at the end of the day but we didn't think that would be too much of an issue as call volumes would be at their lowest for the day. One experienced TM supported by a trusted team captain should be able to see us through till close of business at 22.00.

At 13.00 I got a call from the manager who was scheduled to be on shift from 14.00 until close of play at 10pm. He was sick and there was no way he would make it in to the office that day. Things appeared to be going from bad to worse. However, the change in IVR messaging which pointed callers to the website rather than queue to speak to a customer service adviser seemed to be working. Call delivery was lower than expected and reducing steadily as the day progressed.

We decided that Robbie and I would cover the late shift till 10pm. Robbie was keen to show that he could look after the end of the day on his own but I thought it better that he had some support just in case anything should go wrong. By 8pm things had become ridiculously quiet and I was exhausted having been in the office since half seven in the morning. Robbie was keen to assure me that he could handle things on his own for a couple of hours and that he would contact me if any emergency issues arose. He would also complete and distribute the end of day report which covers final service level numbers and comments around people and behaviours that TMs should be aware of ahead of the weekend. Call volumes were low and Robbie was at the top of his game. What could possibly go wrong?

The first sign that everything wasn't quite as it should be came in the end of day report.

Robbie sent the report exactly as requested but included two pieces of comment that caused me to worry. They were:

- Very busy final hour due to late influx of calls caused by power outage in North Edinburgh reducing SL to 71%
- Pete Stenhouse left the floor one hour before shift end and did not return.

I emailed Robbie's TM to ask her to get to the bottom of why Pete (a highly trusted and capable adviser in his early sixties) would walk off the floor when we were at our busiest and to let me know what Robbie did to support the guys on the floor as the Edinburgh calls started to come through. I decided to call Robbie on the duty mobile to get his views.

To his credit he was still in the office long past the end of his shift and had already called his Team Manager to give her the headlines. In short, we began to receive calls from customers in Edinburgh complaining about a power cut in their area. They couldn't get through on the emergency line so called our Billing number instead. Robbie spoke to the duty manager at our client company who told us that eight thousand households were affected and that engineers were working on the issue now with no estimated time of completion currently available. This is what was agreed we would tell customers who called our billing line. In the meantime, the client's telephony people were putting a message on their IVR to let callers know up front what was happening when they called the correct emergency reporting number. Robbie got our agents together in small groups for a very short period to inform them of the situation and give them the agreed short script.

Up till this point Robbie had performed well so I asked him why he hadn't called me when things started to get extra busy and our service level began to plummet and to tell me a little bit about the Pete situation. He claimed he'd been too busy to call me and that Pete had complained about how stressed he'd been all day and that he'd 'had enough'. I asked Robbie to come in to the office the next morning (Saturday) at 10am for a quick meeting with his TM and myself to help us put together a report for the client and our own client relationship management team who I had called to let them know about the reduction in service and the reason for it.

I went to bed feeling a little uneasy that night. I was kicking myself for not staying in the building with Robbie till the end of shift and the Pete explanation seemed all wrong somehow.

I got in early next morning as I wanted to be there for staff as they arrived and to let TM's know about the power outage and how it may affect the day ahead. Robbie's Team Manager was already at her desk and asked to speak to me privately as soon as I had a moment. I spoke to Client Services who told me the power outage problem had been resolved just before midnight and that call volumes were expected to be back to normal. I let the management team know what I'd been told then asked to speak to Robbie's TM Carol. I could tell by her body language as we walked to a nearby meeting room that she was upset.

Carol is a first rate Team Manager and had prepared superbly for the meeting. I kicked off by asking how she was feeling and did she have any concerns about the day ahead considering she would be the lead TM on shift for most of the day. She had no worries about the day to come but felt she had a great deal she needed to share with me about the final hour of the previous evening's shift. She asked if I would be okay with her showing me a short video clip she had received from an adviser who had been on shift. My heart sank as I knew I wasn't going to like what I was about to see.

What I did see was Robbie and his mate Hugh (another slightly wayward but sometimes brilliant adviser) throwing a kids' basketball to each other from one side of the call floor to the other over the heads of agents taking calls. The time stamp on the video showed 21.35….just when the team was at its busiest handling calls about the power cut. Hugh was actually speaking to customers while standing up and tossing the basketball to his mate – who says men can't multitask?

According to the agent who had filmed the two guys messing around, just after 21.40, the ball struck Pete on the back of the head while he was talking to a customer. Now, Pete is a pretty mild-mannered bloke who likes to just get on with the job and cause as little fuss as possible (I wish there were more like Pete in the contact centre world). However, having a basketball unexpectedly bounce off his nut while he was in the middle of explaining to an angry customer that he couldn't guarantee that power would be restored in time for her to watch The Graham Norton Show at 22.35 was a little too much even for someone as good natured as him so he protested. Here's how that went apparently:

> **Pete:** *What are you doing throwing a ball around when there's so much work to be done?*
> *I just got hit on the head while I was talking to a customer!*
> **Robbie:** *Lighten up Pete we're just having a laugh. (Hugh sniggers in the background).*
> **Pete:** *What do you mean 'lighten up'?*
> *Ya pair of *****! (Pete clearly had the bit between his teeth at this point).*
> *I'll give ye 'lighten up'!*
> *I don't know why they left a clown like you in charge in the first place.*
> *I've had enough!*
> *(Throws down headset, collects coat then leaves the building).*

All of this was very un-Pete like. It was really important that Carol (she was also Pete's TM) should get in touch with him as soon as possible to make sure that he was okay and to let him know we would be taking the situation very seriously and investigating the circumstances ahead of his next planned shift on Monday. He had to be reassured that he was a valued member of the team and that we would do everything in our power to support him in whatever way he felt best. It was crucial that we got him back in the office on Monday as normal or we risked losing him. We also had to hear his side of the story.
In the meantime, we had Robbie to deal with.

Conscious that we could be heading towards a disciplinary investigation and, potentially, a disciplinary hearing I decided to discuss only the service performance aspects of the end of the previous shift. I couldn't be involved in the ball throwing investigation as I would be in line to hear an appeal should the outcome of any initial hearing prove unsatisfactory to Robbie. We also had to arrange for an investigation by his TM into Hugh's part in the affair and I had to stay out of that for similar reasons.

Robbie appeared at exactly 10am. It was his day off so he was doing us a favour just by being there. I explained that Carol and myself wanted to catch up on how things had gone after I left the previous evening, then Carol on her own, would want to talk to him about why Pete had gone home early without permission. He was surprisingly upbeat and had a lot to tell us about how he had dealt with the late influx of emergency calls. It was all very plausible and, to be honest, he'd done a lot of the right things considering he wasn't a trained Team Manager and had little experience of managing a call floor on his own.

I was actually pretty pleased with the actions he had taken and foolishly gave myself a minor pat on the back for agreeing to take a chance on giving him the responsibility in the first place. He'd been put in a difficult position by me and, basketball notwithstanding, had managed things pretty well. In truth I felt a little sorry for him too. He had been trying to do what he thought was right but his tendency toward distraction got the better of him again. It now seemed obvious to me that I had messed up just as much as he had by walking out at 9pm and leaving him to it.

The responsibility had been just too much for someone of Robbie's personality and disposition and I should have anticipated that and taken action to prevent him from reverting to type and doing something silly. I should have stayed the extra hour managing any potential issues as they arose and used Robbie solely to support the floor. I had made a mistake and had to own up to it to HR, my bosses and my management team ahead of any disciplinary investigation.

Carol spoke to both Robbie and Pete and three witnesses who had been on the floor the night of the basketball incident. Robbie was invited to a disciplinary hearing and we changed his shifts for a week to ensure they didn't coincide with Pete's. We also withdrew his secondment pending the outcome of the investigation.

Pete was persuaded to return after personal apologies and assurances from me, Carol and from Robbie.

Robbie turned up for his disciplinary hearing wearing a yellow tartan suit and sporting a Santa Claus tie which played 'Jingle Bells' every time he touched it. Both he and the member of staff he had chosen to accompany him to the hearing sniggered like Beavis and Butthead the whole way through the meeting – especially after Robbie was told about the final formal warning he would receive. On being asked if there was anything further he would like to say or ask, Robbie set off the musical tie again and left the building never to be seen again. No notice of his intention to leave was given and his phone was switched off to prevent us from speaking to him. He was eventually dismissed for being absent without leave.

What a mess.

So, what lessons were learned from this series of situations? What should me and my management team do differently in the future? What would you have done differently if you'd been in our shoes?

Well, both Carol and I have since taken further chances on slightly maverick advisers even after the Robbie thing went wrong. Most have been a success. We tightened up on the expectations and 'dos and don'ts' of all secondments and increased the amount of scrutiny and supervision all secondees received. No-one in that position was ever left solely in charge of the floor even for a few minutes.

Because one individual fails to display what most would regard as reasonable and intelligent behaviours it doesn't follow that similar opportunities should be closed off to enthusiastic people in the future. It is, however, our job as managers to ensure that behavioural expectations are repeatedly made clear to volunteers and that adequate supervision is in place to support the inexperienced when times get tough. As this example clearly shows, if you take your eye off the ball or have unrealistic expectations of staff new to floor management you can easily find yourself in hot water when unfamiliar circumstances present themselves.

Please take time to think about all aspects of this tale: Planning for higher than expected call volumes, higher than usual absence amongst both the agent and manager communities, the relative inexperience of some seconded floor managers and the added stress of the late influx of emergency calls. What will you do (or not do) when some or all of these conditions are presented to you?

Challenging situations rarely appear in isolation when you are a Team Manager. The likelihood is that you may be impacted from a number of directions almost simultaneously. To be effective you have to think ahead. Imagine what difficulties you might find yourself in then plan what you will do should any of these scenarios arise. Who do you need to escalate to? Who will you ask for support? Where can you get the best advice? Who can you pick up the phone to who might act as a second pair of hands if required at short notice? Plan! Plan! Plan!

2 COACHING

What exactly is coaching and why is it so important?

Well, in simple terms, it is the art of improving the performance of others and it's important because, without it, your team members would know nothing more than the little they had been taught in induction training and picked up from listening to the people around them – many of whom are making it up as they go along. Good quality coaching allows your people to develop expertise within their roles and fulfil their potential as individuals. This makes them happy, pleases customers, keeps them engaged within your organisation and prevents them becoming dissatisfied and jumping ship to your competitor's centre in the next town.

Coaching is your opportunity to help your team members achieve their full potential.
Coaching allows you to further enhance your relationship with the people who report to you.
Coaching turns raw material into a business asset.
Coaching builds independence and self-esteem.

Coaching is NOT a one off intervention or event.
Coaching is NOT punishment for underperformance.
Coaching is NOT a tickbox exercise without goals or agreed objectives.
Coaching is NOT a distraction designed to break up the day for managers and advisers alike.

Induction training will give new staff a basic understanding of the job and the tools to scrape their way through non-complex call types. During induction they'll have sat through a bunch of Powerpoint presentations, done a couple of role plays and buddied up on the call floor with a grumpy 'experienced' adviser for a couple of hours on a Friday afternoon because the trainer can't think of what else to do with them and fancies a break before heading to the pub. At the end of two or three weeks trainees will sit a basic evaluation test covering off the stuff in the presentations which was gone over again by the trainer in the last two days of the course....guaranteeing anyone who was even half listening will have a pretty decent chance of scraping a pass. They'll then be released into the wild. This could be straight to their new teams or into a 'nursery' or 'grad bay'. Here some of the nicest people in the building who are aspiring to become trainers or Team Managers will ease them into the world of call handling offering unsustainable levels of support and all round pleasantness in an effort to persuade the new recruits to stay a few weeks longer in the job.

Now I'm not dissing induction training. It is the way it is because traditionally it has been the quickest and most efficient method of getting a group of people of differing abilities to a stage where they may just be able to handle simple calls from undemanding customers without both parties freaking and vowing never to return. No, what bugs me is that the majority of people recruited to call handling positions in contact centres almost certainly didn't do that great at school. They weren't suited to the classroom environment and – as a result – didn't learn or retain very much. Can you see my point?

We take these guys, shove them into another form of classroom and force feed them loads of new information then expect them to create their own system for successfully handling calls from some pretty demanding customers. Is it any wonder that the industry has such a high 90 day attrition rate? In some centres up to half of all new recruits leave the job within the first three months. If you take the time to ask them why they left (something I took the time to do on a number of occasions) they will tell you that the job just 'wasn't for them'. Push them further and you'll get to the truth.

When you speak to people who left the job early without formally resigning – meaning they just decided not to come back and didn't tell anyone they weren't returning – they will give you three main reasons why the work 'wasn't for them'. They are:

1. The job was more complex and challenging than described during the recruitment phase.
2. Induction and on the job training weren't sufficient to allow them to feel competent and comfortable when handling calls.

3. Shift patterns didn't fit with changes in family circumstances and became unsustainable.

Clearly it's for HR, Recruitment and Planning to deal with issues 1 and 3 but the second element of number 2 is firmly on you as Team Manager. So, how do you go about creating a coaching culture within your team that consistently improves the performance of the individual and drives both confidence and engagement?

Getting Started

It's really important that you start as you mean to go on. Coaching is a mindset. By now I'm sure you fully understand that coaching is an on-going relationship and not a single event. Results may take time but each session should drive positive incremental change. Remember that your team member is not a problem to be solved but a person you must take time to understand.

Every adviser must feel that you are on their side rather than on their back. So, what does good coaching look like ?

First, a good coach is a good listener. Giving the coachee the opportunity to speak without interruption or criticism is fundamental to building the relationship of trust required to foster improvement. Coaching is a conversation. **Learn To Listen.**

Second, top coaches ask good questions. Rather than simply telling people what to do they will ask intelligent, pre-prepared questions designed to guide the conversation towards a number of potential actions and solutions. **Ask Good Questions.**

Third, a first rate coach prepares constructive, detailed, high quality feedback designed to support the required change and boost the confidence and self-esteem of the coachee. People tend to take negative criticism personally will make this the focus of any coaching session. Good coaches understand this so tend to use positive language and deliver only **Constructive Feedback.**

Fourth, great coaches generate great ideas. As they build experience they create a bank of ideas that they know will work in given situations. They use these ideas sparingly and as jumping off points when conversations become stagnant or the individual being coached doesn't quite know where to go next. Great coaches are always able to **Generate Creative Ideas.**

Don't Re-Invent The Wheel

Taking into account everything I've just told you about what great coaching looks like I'd like to now present you with the world's simplest coaching plan to help you get started in this most crucial aspect of your role. Get this part right and you'll be already be a better performer than 50% of your colleagues. It's deliberately not complex in any way but covers all the basics of what's required.

1. **Get your mindset right.** Decide that your approach will be to develop an obviously supportive coaching culture within your team. Fill every spare minute with positive side-by-side and remote sessions delivering helpful, confidence-building support to all of your team members. Make a positive coaching environment the hallmark of your team 'brand'. Only your energy and positivity will make this happen.
2. **Set The Tone From Day One.** Conduct an 'entrance interview' with all new members of the team. Let them know what your expectations are and how you will support them through coaching to achieve these. Give them the opportunity to set their own first 90 day goals and objectives and jointly agree the roadmap that will take them there. Let them know how passionate you are about coaching and follow-up on the planned coaching schedule exactly as agreed. Don't allow yourself to become distracted to the extent that the coaching schedule slips and your team loses faith in your ability to deliver.

A Simple Case Example

Observation showed that many of the staff on a newly outsourced energy billing project had yet to get to grips with navigating through the various screens of the client company's billing system. Some were also very unclear on some of the key processes they should follow when, for example, a business customer called to change a property address or to cancel an account and open a new one in another name.

'First Call Resolution' percentage was down at 71% against a contractual target of 92%. This meant that almost three out of every ten callers were calling back within fourteen days to raise the same queries again. Needless to say this represents poor customer service and is an unnecessary cost to both the client and outsource businesses. It also meant a quality fail for each call handler.

Combined data from telephony and the proprietary billing system allowed operational managers, L&D and the quality monitoring team to identify which customers had called back and which agents had handled the initial calls. The call recordings were pulled and a massive listening exercise began. The purpose being to try to identify where the worst offending advisers were going wrong compared to those who had strong FCR numbers and who followed the agreed call 'roadmap'.

The exercise threw up a few very clear issues including:

- Persistent hesitation and silences when attempting to navigate the system.
- Uncertainty of tone when delivering answers to very specific queries.
- Answering questions with irrelevant information because the adviser felt they were perhaps on more solid ground by regurgitating the small number of general things they did know and understand.
- No attempt to clarify the customer's query at the start of the call.
- No attempt to summarise actions taken by the adviser at the end of the call.
- Failure to ask the customer if there was anything further they required help with.
- A very small number of advisers were causing the majority of the repeat calls.

It was obvious that immediate action would have to be taken to close off each of the issues identified in the listening exercise. So, a corrective action plan was drawn up and each of the interested stakeholder groups (Operations/Training/Quality) took on designated responsibilities.

It was decided that each Team Manager would coach their two worst performing team members in using the correct call openings and closings and ensure 100% compliance around these within the remainder of their team group.

Team Manager Alison could see from reports that she had two direct reports who were clearly failing on FCR. She arranged with the real time management team what she could have 30 minute individual sessions with Iain and Derek her poor performers. Alison explained to the two guys why they were meeting, showed them evidence of the issue and agreed coaching plans for each. She also asked them to commit to turn each coaching point into an action on all calls going forward. In the meantime, the training department would support with group sessions covering system navigation and the most commonly misunderstood processes. Alison would follow up with coaching on those areas when she was satisfied that Iain and Derek were opening and closing all calls according to the agreed call script.

Improvement in FCR can be a bit of a pain to coach as you cannot see the results in terms of numbers until at least 14 days has passed – sometimes even longer as this report is not usually one that is published daily or even weekly. However, Alison put together a five point coaching plan that would allow her to track the extent to which Iain and Derek had developed the correct call handling habits. She had faith that getting the guys to do the correct things on all calls would drive the improvements she required.

The plan was simple and this was it:

1. Explain to Iain and Derek what the issue is and how it could be fixed. Play them the beginnings and endings of their calls where script had not been followed. Find out why they were failing to follow the script. Address any fears they may have.
2. Ensure they fully understand which elements of the script could not be missed and let them hear what 'good' sounds like. Play recorded examples of calls by other agents where correct opening and close were included effectively.
3. Plan two 30 minute side-by-side coaching sessions listening to Iain and Derek using the correct opening and close on all calls and having conversations about where improvements may be required.
4. Complete a daily remote listening session to take in live or recorded calls from both advisers and ensure opening and close was used correctly on all calls. Follow up with short five minute side-by-side sessions to recognise improvement and offer further advice where required.
5. Continue to sporadically dip into call recordings to be assured of continued compliance then feed back and congratulate on any improvement when reporting becomes available. Continually praise and thank the two advisers for their efforts.

Alison combined this plan with extra sessions being run by the L and D team designed to help the entire adviser community improve their system, product and process knowledge.

After four weeks of coaching and training FCR improved across the floor from 71% to 83%. It was then decided that TMs should focus all their coaching efforts on the single poorest performer in each of their teams. In a very small number of cases very weak *performers were moved to an easier campaign as it was felt they may never achieve the required standard in a fairly complex billing related role.*

The key to Alison's success in this instance is that she focussed on only one area of improvement and created a simple coaching plan and followed it through to completion. She requested the support of L and D and the real time management teams which helped her plan time off calls for the two guys and made sure that their other areas of weakness would be addressed by a trainer. She didn't let the every-day contact centre noise and interference get in her way and was prepared to give her own time outside her shift to get into a room and listen to calls or prepare paperwork.

This kind of coaching approach can be used on any number of issues from AHT to customer service skills. It's crucially important to keep the message simple and to assure yourself that the coachee is using your advice immediately and on all appropriate calls.

Top quality coaching will deliver positive, fast improvements in your team performance. Please keep it simple by focussing each adviser on one small change in their call-handling behaviour at a time. Always let them see or hear what 'great' looks like by playing them lots of excellent examples then follow up by checking their work daily to ensure that the last coaching message has got through and is now embedded in every appropriate customer interaction.

There are as many coaching techniques as there are managers but I'm conscious that new TMs in particular may require a few little ideas to help get them started or to freshen up a stagnating approach. Try these:

1. If you give struggling agents too much to think about they'll become overwhelmed. Give each member of your team one thing only to improve on over a prescribed five working-day period. Keep it ridiculously simple – something like increasing the number of 'please' and 'thank you' responses used in each call. Monitor and check the improvement then publicly congratulate the agent.
2. At quiet points in the day pair up your advisers and let them listen to each other's calls then give positive feedback to their buddy on what they liked best about their approach. Good habits will rub off.
3. Plan an hour two afternoons a week when you will walk around wearing a headset randomly plugging in beside each of your guys at

the start of calls. Be super positive about the good things you hear. It's all about reinforcement.
4. Group together agents who are struggling in one aspect of their call handling and charge them with collectively improving and developing their skills in that area. Have them report back to you the actions taken and results observed. Take time to listen to the group's calls to ensure the correct methods and behaviours have in face been embedded.

Most importantly – irrespective of which method of coaching you decide to use – whether it's sitting beside your people and supporting in real-time, listening remotely then following up with a five minute 121 session or in a group live learning environment the crucial point is this:

Successful coaching outcomes are only achieved when the message being delivered is simplified and reduced to one single key concept. Most advisers in a live environment can only focus on introducing one new idea into their call-handling armoury at a time. Remove all complexity from your coaching messages. Leave no room for confusion.

3 BUILDING ENGAGEMENT

Over the years I've probably spent more hours in meetings discussing employee engagement than on any other topic. Businesses and organisations worldwide recognise that the extent to which an individual is 'engaged' with her work will determine how productive that person is and will be a significant factor in any decision made by that employee on whether to move to another role and company. However, the same organisations are finding it increasingly difficult to build the kinds of corporate 'culture' which promote high levels of engagement and productivity and reduce attrition (turnover or leavers) to an absolute minimum.

So, what's a decent definition of Employee Engagement? For this kind of thing I like to turn to the Chartered Institute of Personnel and Development – or CIPD for short - who are a much trusted source of education and practical information on the subject of managing staff. They're current definition of 'Employee Engagement' within the workplace is:

Being positively present during the performance of work by willingly contributing intellectual effort, experiencing positive emotions and meaningful connections to others.

You know already how I like to simplify things down to a couple of simple phrases so I'm not going to disappoint you now. For me engagement is feeling happy and comfortable in the workplace while being sufficiently stimulated by the work you're being asked to perform. As a Team Manager I don't believe you need to think more strategically than this. Your job is to create an environment within your team that promotes general feelings of happiness and comfort for each of your team members while ensuring that all of your staff remain stimulated and stretched by the work you're asking them to do.

If you succeed in this you will be in the fortunate position of having the most productive group in your business together with the lowest staff turnover numbers. Let me assure you, these are the kinds of things that will get you noticed by senior management and opens doors to all sorts of career opportunities. However, I've no intention of downplaying how time-consuming and challenging it can be to create an engaged culture. It's damn hard work. Some people don't want to be engaged and will resist and undermine you at every opportunity. Others may never have experienced what it feels like to enjoy work and the workplace so will find it difficult to trust you and your intentions.

Persistence will be the key to your success in this. Get your head down and keep going through all the obstacles and roadblocks that are put in front of you. Decide what your engaged team will look like and make it happen step by tiny step. Plan your roadmap and follow through on all of your micro tasks and mini intentions. Show the naysayers that you will bulldoze your way through their energy sapping negativity and that your will to create something good, worthwhile and sustainable is far greater that theirs. It will be exhausting at times but worth it in the end.

Improving staff engagement at business or organisation level can be a massive piece of work where all departments become joined up in their intentions. Management styles and approaches will alter and become more consistent as part of what can be a long-term plan.

Why do staff become disengaged in the first place? Even worse, why do some staff _never_ engage with their employer or the role they've been employed to do? What is it about some workplaces that prevents good people - who have often been hired at great expense - from committing to the work and colleagues they enthusiastically applied to join? What happens in the period between the excitement of being offered a wonderful new job within what looks like a great place to work and the point where the same individual has become disillusioned to the point they cannot bear to continue to turn up and be part of what they have come to perceive as a disinterested, underwhelming and unrewarding environment no longer worthy of their continued enthusiasm and good intentions?

To be absolutely frank with you, most contact centre employers who fail to engage the majority of their staff do so for the same old reasons. Annual employee engagement and staff surveys tell a major part of the story. And, if you want to get to the very heart of the issue then it's worth tracking down some of the people who have left your organisation without notice (or attending the almost useless standard exit interview) as many will be only too delighted to tell you why the job 'just wasn't for them'. The truth is out there but few senior management teams have the time, money or people resources required to address the bigger issues that are consistently raised in annual surveys. Changing a failing culture can be just too big a job so often they will decide to manage disaffection, absence and attrition as best they can rather than tackling what is at the root of their problems.

In no particular order here are just some of the reasons for low levels of engagement that come up time and time again in staff engagement surveys. It should be said that third party run outsourced centres tend to have poorer scores than longer established in-house or insourced projects and campaigns. Higher rates of pay, increased numbers of opportunities to progress and more convenient shift patterns are just some of the reasons that established, proprietary business areas tend to score better and, importantly, promote longer tenure within the relatively unskilled agent communities:

- Low rates of pay
- Unsustainable shift patterns/too many weekends
- Too many short-notice changes to established shift rota
- Few opportunities for development and advancement
- Inadequate training and coaching
- Team Managers are unskilled, untrained and don't seem to care
- Senior management team is totally detached from agents on the call floor
- Feedback and communication across the centre are inconsistent or non-existent
- Compulsory job description changes at short notice e.g. service to sales
- Lack of recognition for a job well done
- HR policies on lateness and attendance too strict and unreasonable
- Staff not valued by managers
- 121s and meetings cancelled without notice
- Unclear view of what the job actually is and where it fits in bigger picture

- Sales and AHT targets too difficult to achieve
- Systems too slow adding to AHT and customer dissatisfaction
- Poor sound quality on telephone lines causing customer dissatisfaction
- Managers don't acknowledge team members other than their 'favourites'
- Not enough free parking spaces
- Persistent payroll errors e.g. overtime payments delayed for months without reason or notice
- Sausages in cafeteria are rubbish

Quite a list isn't it? I promise you that some of these perceptions currently apply to you, your TM colleagues and your business as a whole. It's time to do something about it don't you think?

Don't give too much thought to the larger, organisation-wide challenges. I'm sure you'll have your opportunity to contribute to a bigger debate once you've made some inroads into your more immediate concerns.

I want you to focus on what can be done at an individual and team level. Ignore what's happening at senior management level – their behaviours are for them to consider and improve if that's what is required…..you can lead by example. Get your blinkers on and concentrate on how you can engage every member of the team that reports to you. Can I suggest that you take time to find material that takes a more detailed look at improving engagement at a more macro level but, for now, here are a few practical ideas to help you kick off your team member engagement improvement plan.

Let me warn you that you're going to be tempted to throw down this book in outrage (be careful if you're reading the digital edition on your phone!!!). Your first reaction to what comes next is likely to be something along the lines of 'This guy must think I'm an idiot….I do all of this really basic stuff every day and don't need to be told. It's just common sense'. Bear with me – there's method behind what seems like over simplification.

I often hold skip level meetings with agents where their TMs are not present. I arrange a lunch and ask a dozen or so people from across all teams on the floor to join me for a general chat around what we're doing well and what we could be doing better. It never ceases to amaze me the level of insight that is shown at these sessions and I never fail to come away with lots of really strong and sometimes surprising information relating to how agents feel they are being managed. I must also say that the same things come up time and time again and these form the basis of my simple guide to improving engagement within the adviser community.

So, when I'm holding monthly individual 121s with Team Managers and they are 'insulted' when I offer my very basic ideas on how they can further engage their team members, I am able to produce the verbatim evidence of my skip levels (no agent names mentioned of course) to support my belief that the basics aren't always being adhered to.

I promise you this isn't some kind of childish management trick or power trip to trap a manager into a position where I can prove them wrong and put them on the back foot. In fact, I always share the headlines from my agent sessions with all of the managers in my teams, my boss and with the head of HR in order that they have a temperature check of how the people on our floor might be feeling at given points throughout the year. An informal employee engagement survey, if you like, which guarantees no surprises when the official annual survey time comes around. It also allows TMs to get a regular generalised view, as a group, of how their people perceive them.

Incidentally, at each agent session I capture a minimum of three of their concerns that I believe I can have an immediate impact on…..we call them 'quick-wins' and I promise to get back to all attendees as soon as I can with the outcomes of any actions I've taken away with me. This, in itself, builds confidence in the value of the sessions and, in a small way, contributes to strengthening feelings of engagement. Try this as a part of your own team meetings but be careful not to promise what you can't deliver as this may damage your team's confidence in your abilities.

Now – back to what you can do to improve the sense of engagement within your team. It's pretty safe to say that all of what follows describes things that were raised in the agent sessions as being essential but didn't seem to be happening universally across all teams and all staff.

First, ensure that each team member has had a 'welcome interview' either when they first join your team or when you initially take over the group. Sessions should last 15-30 minutes and should cover things like:

- Did training meet your expectations? If not, what can be done now to close the gaps?
- Has someone gone over what we do here and how the work you do fits in?
- What do you want to get out of your time with the organisation? What are your ambitions?
- How can I, as your TM, help you achieve your goals?
- Gently discover what you can about the agent's interests and background as a person
- Describe your team culture and how you see it developing
- Manage expectations regarding lateness/absence reporting and leave requests
- Make a promise to be available for them whenever they need support
- Create a joint plan regarding how you will help them integrate quickly

It's important to take notes throughout this interview and to refer to them as part of the monthly performance management process and to support the informal work you will do with each individual every day as you attempt to build the kind of manager/agent relationship that promotes superior levels of commitment and productivity. A strong personal relationship of this kind quickly becomes one of the fundamental 'hooks' that bind people to organisations and makes them think twice before leaving to start again elsewhere.

Second, you will find it hard to believe the number of times I've been told by agents that they have been consistently 'ignored' by their manager…sometimes for days on end. In fact, I once spoke to an adviser who had yet to meet his Team Manager even though he had been in the business and handling calls for three months! (Totally unacceptable and no excuses but almost understandable due to a unique series of events involving an early move from full-time induction training on to a unique part-time late evening shift pattern followed by two badly communicated quick fire moves to new teams and a Team Manager who went off on leave then long-term sick and returned on a phased day-shift basis!!)

You will not be surprised to learn how much resentment and dissatisfaction can build as a result of these kinds of circumstances.

Most people don't want too much attention from their boss. They simply want to be acknowledged in a friendly and civil way and to know that their manager will be there for them on the rare occasion that they need her to be. A casual and informal greeting at the start of the agent or manager's shift and a 'see you tomorrow' at the end of the day is the very least an employee should expect but I believe you would be totally amazed at the extent to which this <u>does not</u> happen or, at least is perceived by some agents not to happen often enough.

It's my belief that managers rarely consciously ignore members of staff. What is more likely is that they become totally immersed in the urgent tasks of the day that continuously present themselves and simply forget to acknowledge people as they arrive to begin their shift or are in meetings or on calls when staff leave at the end of the day. There is so much goodwill to be gained, however, by getting into the excellent habit of ensuring that you greet and wave-off every individual in as personal way as you can. Use their names, mention something relevant to them (traffic jams where they live, kids getting to school ok, football or Eastenders on TV tonight etc)…..anything at all that shows an interest in them as individuals.

These are also perfect opportunities to deliver one simple work-related message that is designed to make them feel good about themselves and support targeted improvements. Here are a few slightly naff sounding examples. Think about what I'm trying to get across to you and change the wording as you see fit to suit your personality:

- 'Five upsales yesterday Johnny-boy – brilliant! Any chance of six to-day? (Laugh)'
- 'Just seen your Quality scores for the month Michelle. Amazing again! Will catch up this afternoon at two. Well done.'
- 'See you in the morning Steve. By the way, just listened to the call you had with Mr Francis this afternoon. Don't know how you managed to keep your temper with him – he was really challenging. Well done. Do you mind if I use that call for training the new guys on how to deal with difficult customers? Really, really good. Cheers!'
- 'Did you get Mrs Newman sorted ok Shaz? I wasn't really sure what she was looking for, were you? You sounded like you knew what you were talking about though! (smile). You're off till Monday aren't you? Enjoy your weekend. Doing anything special? Have a good one.'

Now I know these kinds of contrived conversations can appear unnatural when you see them written in black and white. I also know that the language I use is going to be different to the stuff you say to your colleagues when you're in the office. My point, however, is simply that too many individuals who work in the lowest paid roles within contact centres believe that their manager really doesn't care very much about them and is unlikely to make an authentic and genuine effort to communicate with them on a human level and that is a crime in my view.

A minute spent at the beginning and end of each shift with <u>every</u> member of the team – be careful not to miss anyone out or you'll breed resentment – will pay rich dividends in the long run. If you are on a call or in a meeting then try to wave or signal some form of acknowledgement or recognition. This could be one of the most important habits you ever develop.

Listen – I appreciate that it can be awkward trying to make friendly conversation with a 62 year old retired policeman when you've only just got your first manager's job at the age of 23. His interests are more likely to be around things like family, holidays and gardening rather than clubbing, drinking and eating junk food (apologies for both obvious age related stereotypes). He will tell you that he is doing the job to make a little money over and above his Police pension and to fill some of his time while using his brain because he's too young and active to sit and do nothing. You, on the other hand, are now on the first rung of the corporate ladder. A potential thrusting executive with a successful career in front of you. What can you possibly talk to him about on a daily basis that won't sound trite and patronising?

Simple. Just take a little time to get to know him. Ask about how he spends his time when he's not working and share some of the things you do too. Build a relationship based on what you learn about each other. Notice when he's not on top form and make yourself available for a chat if you feel that's what he wants but don't push or you may find yourself embarrassed by his 'what would you know?' reaction to you. Be authentic. Take a genuine interest.

People management should be a gentle and subtle activity. Nudging and supporting your team members into the best place for both your business and them as individuals will be far more successful than trying to force your will upon them. Remember that you will learn more from the people you manage that they ever will from you.

Show your team the respect they deserve. Renew your connections with them every day. Recognise that each of us is a human being with a complicated and challenging life. Respect employees as equals and let them know you have their best interests at heart. Do not let a day go by where you haven't welcomed every team member to the office and caught up with them just before they leave (shift allowing). At quiet points in the day go round and spend a couple of minutes with everyone in the group and chat – it doesn't all have to be work related. Show the human touch every day without fail and you'll be well on the way to being perceived as a strong manager of people. Do it because most other managers don't and staff engagement suffers as a result. Most of all, do it because it's simply the right thing to do.

Next I'd like you to look closely at how you communicate with your team both as a group and as individuals. This one comes up in almost every survey of staff engagement and never seems to go away unless it becomes a priority focus at manager and business levels. Frankly, the only way to give yourself a chance of stopping this being an on-going issue is to let all staff know that you have accepted their feedback about the style and inadequacy of current communications. Take time at a team meeting to discuss your comms improvement plan and ask them to judge your progress once a month at designated team meetings.

If you make genuine progress then that will be agreed and underlined at your group discussions leaving little room for complaint come annual staff satisfaction survey time. You must own the plan and the improvement because no-one will do it for you. If you let the whole thing run out of steam you will lose the respect and trust of your team members and they may not take seriously any similar future initiative.

Here are a few simple actions you can build your comms improvement plan around:

1. **Hold daily buzz meetings or team huddles.** Five minute sessions at the start of each shift covering the day's priorities together with an overview of the previous day's performance at team level. Set targets for the coming day and ask for questions that should be addressed quickly. These mini team meetings must

be exclusively positive in tone and mustn't be allowed to turn into a moan 'fest'.
2. **Target vulnerable individuals for support and feedback.** Identify one or two team members at risk of struggling during the next few hours. It may be they have just returned to work after a period of sickness or simply that they have performed poorly recently due to personal issues. Help them to feel good about themselves and let them know they have your full confidence. Be certain that they are aware of any product, process or systems changes that may have been announced during their absence.
3. **Make team meetings count.** Ensure you have an agenda and minutes for every meeting. Be prepared to share information related to your wider business and clients as this promotes a feeling of belonging to something bigger and more dynamic rather than just being part of a small, insular group and performing the same few tasks day after day. Please check with your boss and HR before you share anything sensitive that could potentially cause unrest. Do not cancel a planned meeting unless it is absolutely necessary. If cancellation is unavoidable then get a new time and date in the diary as soon as possible and communicate to all team members with your apologies. Let them know that you take team meetings very seriously indeed.
4. **Make sure 121s go ahead as planned.** For many staff members the monthly 121 is the only chance they have to spend private, personal time with their line manager. It is their single four-weekly opportunity to express their thoughts on the role, the team and the business as a whole. It's your job as TM to listen to what they have to say and address their concerns. Prepare well and have all the required numbers to hand for discussion. Bear in mind that, although the monthly 121 forms part of the performance management process, a great deal can also be achieved around heading off any potential personal issues as well as uncovering opportunities to boost levels of engagement. Above all, take an interest and make every effort to communicate that you see these meetings as being of crucial importance in supporting the agent's career aspirations and enjoyment of the role. Agree actions to be followed up at the next monthly 121 and to be discussed as part of your daily, floor-based, five-minute catch-ups. Again, if cancellation is unavoidable, get a new date and time in the diary that suits both parties and pull out all the stops to make certain that it takes place.

Take time to recognise a job well done. Work at catching people doing things right rather than finding fault all the time. Everyone does something well. Find out what that is and dish out the praise at an appropriate point. Don't become the kind of ineffective manager who takes pride in withholding pats on the back in an effort to be seen as a 'hard taskmaster'. It's not clever and can make you look like an immature fool who is on some kind of power trip. The best managers know when to commend their team and aren't shy in doing so.

One final word on successful communications.

Many inexperienced Team Managers find the temptation to trade business 'secrets' with their friends or favourite team members almost irresistible. As you move into your first junior management role you find yourself party to a great deal of business-sensitive information that you simply wouldn't have been exposed to in previous positions. This brings with it the responsibility to think professionally about who this should and should not be shared with.

The best managers are always conservative in their handling of what is often a combination of fact and rumour. They know that idle chat with their mates in the agent community can cause major problems further down the line if what you've shared is later taken out of context or, more likely, twisted into something very different from the original conversation.

Employee relations can be volatile and sensitive at the best of times. This is especially so in a unionised environment where it is the duty of union officials to address with senior management any hint of possible changes of policy that reach them through the rumour mill. So much unnecessary heartache can be avoided if junior managers can learn when to keep their mouths shut about something they may have heard in passing at a meeting where the organisation's decision makers have been holding court.

In my experience, Team Managers who try to buy respect from the agent community in the pub on a Friday night by having a 'Look, I really shouldn't be telling you this but……' type of conversation soon find themselves in hot water and very quickly placed on the Not To Be Trusted list that senior managers keep tucked away in the backs of their minds. Careers can be ended all too soon through careless talk. My advice to you is this – share nothing informally…keep it all to yourself until you have permission to communicate to the wider community. That way you can sleep easily when the inevitable witch hunt begins after the Managing Director has been chinned by the Staff Rep Council team about something somebody was told by a manager in the pub at the weekend about a department being closed and the work moved offshore.

Poor communication can be worse than no communication at all. Learn when to say nothing.

As a rule, it's better for managers not to get involved in tittle-tattle and unsubstantiated rumour and hearsay. Be careful around what you communicate and to whom. Stick to the publicly available facts and the company line would be my advice.

4 PERFORMANCE MANAGEMENT

I once put myself forward for a manager's role with a large utilities company. It seemed to offer more opportunities for career development than the outsourced environment I had begun my contact centre life within. It also paid more money for what appeared to be an almost identical job description.

Anyway, I was looking forward to the interview as it would give me a chance to show off the wonderful knowledge and skills I believed I had built up in the three years I had been working with a number of big name organisations who had outsourced their customer service functions to us. One of the first questions I was asked at the interview was this:

'What is your preferred model of performance management?'

Looking back I was incredibly naïve. I genuinely believed that my little outsourced world had all the answers and led the way in delivering superior performance in a dynamic and fast-moving industry. My business related terminology and vocabulary – such as it was – had been developed exclusively in that arena and guess what? 'Performance Management' (PM) was not a term we used every day on our call floor to describe how we measured performance and energized and motivated employees to deliver value to our business and those of our clients.

So, in terms of the interview question, I was stumped. Not only was I unsure of the meaning of the term, I also had no clue as to what the range of models available to me actually were. I scrambled together a response covering methods used to achieve contractual SLAs and what action I would take if we discovered we were failing….a load of waffle frankly. The utilities company's interview panel saw straight through me and I was politely shown the door. Needless to say I didn't get the job.

Once the cringe and embarrassment of that event had worn off I immediately set out to learn as much as I could about Performance Management and how it is applied in the big, wide world outside my little centre in the West of Scotland. I was surprised to learn that I did, in fact, already know a great deal about the subject and was working to a recognised if somewhat hybrid model. Appraisals, objectives, 121s, KPIs etc……all were second nature to me but I didn't at that point understand that each of these more than familiar terms fell under the umbrella of 'Performance Management'.

Now, I know that you are much better informed than I was back then. I'm aware that you will immediately recognise the term 'Performance Management' and how it applies to your working life. However, for the sake of clarity, let me spell out what it means to me in the simplest terms possible. I'll then go ahead and give you an easy to use approach which you can combine with your business's requirements that will guarantee you get off to the best possible start while ticking all the relevant boxes to the satisfaction of all stakeholders (agent, manager, HR, business).

For decades managers have perceived their role in managing performance as being the curator of key stats, the facilitator of annual staff appraisals and the communicator of performance appraisal ratings to the wider business. Throw in a brief discussion around objectives for the coming year and that just about covers it for the next twelve months.

Now, that approach may have worked briefly for a short period – probably in 1973 or then abouts - but things have moved on significantly. Businesses and employees alike now expect a much more empathetic, detailed, two-way, on-going conversation to take place throughout the year supporting staff in understanding where the work they do fits in the whole jigsaw of service delivery and successful business performance.

Since as long ago as 2002 world renowned companies decided that an annual one-off, top-down, one-way conversation often perceived as an intervention rather than as part of a holistic programme of planned support and motivation really was so last century in the contemporary, forward-thinking workplace.

They decided to move towards a performance management environment that was employee-centred rather than organisation-centred, focussed on outcomes rather than outputs and continuous development as opposed to individual feedback delivered just once or twice a year.

'Control' would be a thing of the past and replaced with emotionally intelligent and appropriate forms of motivation. The wellbeing of the employee would be at the core of the process and a fundamental responsibility of the employer.

They began to speak of OKRs (Mutually Agreed Objectives and Key Results) rather than MBOs (Management By Organisation-Defined Objectives) and KPIs. OKRs rely on SMART goals where individualised objectives are agreed as part of a joint agreement between employee and employer.

However, for far too many managers and their staff the words 'performance management' still mean pain. The general understanding remains that an annual or six-monthly appraisal will take place using whatever numbers the manager can scrape together. Multiple forms will be filled in and a few vague objectives agreed after which the whole lot will be dumped in the employee management system overseen by the Human Resources team. An overall performance score for each individual may or may not play some part in determining the level of any annual salary increase awarded to those with the highest ratings.

In some organisations, what I've described above will be the full extent of PM activities. As far as they are aware no obvious effort to improve staff morale and motivation will have been made yet management and HR will sit back in their executive chairs satisfied that they can tick the box that states that this type of exercise should take place at the same time every year using exactly the same methodology irrespective of its perceived effectiveness.

It will be unclear that any attempt to express and describe the work of each employee as part of a bigger picture will have been made yet Team Managers will breathe a sigh of relief that this load of nonsense is over for another year and they can stop panicking about the lack of numbers and evidence they've been able to put together to support their gut feelings about how the people in their teams have been getting on. The amount of effort, activity, paperwork and worry that has to go into annual appraisal time can be genuinely overwhelming for an inexperienced Team Manager so getting the whole thing over and done with can be something of a relief.

Most agents will come out the other side of their annual appraisal feeling vaguely dissatisfied at the outcome but relieved that it's over and glad that they can forget about it until the same time next year. They'll leave with a written record of what they achieved in the previous year together with a bunch of numbers they must aim to hit over the next twelve months. But will they have any sense of how to achieve their new objectives and do they understand how what they do contributes to the goals of the company? Probably not in my view.

Let me ask you now – as a forward thinking manager who is determined to drive maximum value from every process and interaction – can you see how a different approach could potentially stimulate greater performance, commitment and engagement? I certainly can and I'm going to set it out for you in this section.

First, my usual warning to you. If you leave all of your planning and data collection till the last minute you will drown. You will almost certainly require the support of your colleagues in your company's management information reporting teams to help you out and you should bear in mind that they will be supporting all other managers in the same way at the same time so you must ensure that you're not at the end of the queue when formally requesting that they do some work on your behalf. If your business operates a support request ticketing system then follow that process to the letter and take time to word your requirements in a way that is easily understood. If the MI guys have to keep reverting to you for further clarification and explanation you will very soon find yourself at the back of their queue and scrambling for time as deadline day approaches.

Better still, learn how to extract relevant data and run and automate reports without the need for third party support. Teaching yourself these skills will make life so much easier as all the agent and team level MI you will ever need will be at your fingertips at the drop of a hat and the reporting team will love you when their workload is reduced as you become self-sufficient. (Just make sure you have permission to run your own customised reports and that you aren't in any way interfering with other business crucial MI).

Okay, let's assume you know how to put together all the performance related stats you'll ever need to support the PM process. What are the next steps?

As usual, let's agree to keep this whole Performance Management thing as simple as possible while ensuring that our activities in this discipline will be fully effective. We will define PM – for you as Team Manager – as the accumulation of actions taken to ensure that each of your agents successfully contributes to the goals and and objectives of the organisation you work for.

Think solely in terms of these three constituent parts and you won't go far wrong:

- Mutually Agreed Outcome Related Objectives
- Tailored Continuous Improvement
- Joint Accountability

That's it – nothing more. Don't confuse yourself by trying to develop or implement a more technical or complex approach.

So, each of your team members should participate in a formal monthly 121 meeting with their line manager and an annual or half-yearly discussion and assessment of their recent performance in meetings most often called 'appraisals'. The annual sessions are the biggies because this is when actual performance will be formally compared to the objectives you mutually agreed at the beginning of the twelve month period just passed. This is why you as their TM will have to collect and present the relevant data as this constitutes the information required to measure actual performance against goals.

An overall score for the agent's year will be arrived at using a standardised method for evaluating her contribution to the business over the last twelve months. This number may then go on to be used to trigger incremental increases in salary assuming an agreed threshold has been achieved.

I've deliberately made all of this sound a bit formal because this is an area you cannot afford to mess around in. People's careers and salaries are determined by the work you do around this. Often, your first attempt at scoring and determining any potential salary increase will have to be reviewed due to budget restrictions. This can be pretty upsetting for any individual who justifiably believes they should have received a higher performance rating that the one they actually received.

A few years ago I was part of a group charged with bringing together the annual appraisal scores and ratings for every member of staff in our branch of the business for whom we worked – that was around 800 people. We then had to distribute the allocated budget for annual salary increases and bonuses in a way that rewarded the best performers and motivated those who weren't far from achieving the top rating. This proved pretty challenging to do as the company wanted us to operate a very simple rating system where the best guys would be rated a '3', the massive moderately performing group at '2' and the guys who required further development (or were just a bit rubbish and didn't care at all about how they performed) at '1'.

Having decided on agreed bonus and salary increase amounts we found the budget would allow us only to rate 20% of staff at Level 3, 60% at Level 2 and the guys who achieved a rating of '1' also had to make up 20% of total staff numbers. Unfortunately, line managers had already rated 28% of their people at 3, 70% at 2 and just 12% at 1. Even though the managers' original ratings had not been communicated to staff it left us all in a bit of a predicament as almost 18% of our total staff community would have to have their original scores reduced to meet the available budget. Managers were understandably furious as they believed they had submitted accurate and fair ratings during the appraisal process and were of the opinion that awarding a large number of employees with less than they deserved would prove to be massively demotivating. I suspected they may be right.

So, we asked the management team to look again at their scoring and create subgroups which we would term as 'Lower 3' and 'Lower 2'. We considered altering the rating system to accommodate five groups rather than three and re-allocating the budget accordingly. This was rejected at board level as too much of a departure from what staff had been used to over the years and HR believed that we would have had to communicate the change in rating system prior to appraisals taking place. They thought that it wouldn't look good to announce a new scoring system after the event possibly giving rise to suspicions of reverse engineering subsequent to the results having been collated and awards calculated.

There was only one thing for it – line managers would have to find sufficient numbers of people from within their teams to reduce to the lower appraisal grade. As you can imagine, this caused plenty of heartache. Each manager was told to look again at their appraisals and subsequent awards then come back with 20% of their team rated as '3',

60% as '2' and the remainder as '1'. I can all too easily imagine that some managers would have elected to reduce the scores of their team members least likely to kick up a fuss or who they didn't like as much as someone of equal score who they had more time for. To make matters worse, 9 months later we had to make a number of redundancies and those who had been rated at '1' were first in the firing line. A double dollop of unfairness landed on those we had had to reduce from a 2 to a 1 just to fit the amount in the previous year's bonus pot.

I've recounted this little tale in an effort to get the message across to you that performance management can become a minefield if you don't approach it as an everyday activity. Throwing numbers and messages together once a year at the last minute simply won't work if you genuinely want to drive superior performance, hang onto your best people and also satisfy the ever-growing hunger for relevant business information and data. Both you and your team members must have a crystal clear understanding of where their standard of performance measured against implicitly understood agreed objectives is sitting on any given day of the year. In simple terms, all staff should be aware of how their performance in work is currently rated by management at all times and not learned as part of a six-monthly or annual appraisal process.

My advice to you on managing performance comes to you in three basic parts and is designed to be simple, easy to follow and as all encompassing as I can make it. Most importantly, try to ensure that both the staff member and the business you work for are at the heart of everything you do on this. Employees in 2021 demand more and better communication and expect their voices to be heard while businesses require thoroughness, empathy and fairness to be demonstrably at the core of how their performance management policy and process is delivered by first-line managers.

First, become expert in all elements of your employer's performance management policies and processes. You really need to know what your business expects of you in this aspect of your role as Team Manager. Familiarise yourself with all the relevant on-line forms and databases, rating systems, definitions of possible objectives, key delivery dates and escalation routes should you run into trouble. Ask your HR account manager to show you best practice examples and create a template and checklist for you to follow. This way you can be sure of covering everything off in a timely fashion without fear of missing anything then subsequently presenting all related 'paperwork' in the kind of professional format you already know will be well received by both the business and the staff member.

Second, accept that performance management is a 365 days a year activity and not simply a twice-yearly intervention imposed on the people in your team. If you are doing your job properly you will briefly speak to every member of your group individually at some point during their daily shift to discuss their previous day's numbers and what you expect of each other during the next eight hours or so. The subjects you cover should align to objectives agreed at appraisals and monthly 121s. These objectives are not just a wish list you get together twice a year to talk about then pay scant attention to for the other 363 days. They must have a relevance to every hour of every day of an employee's existence within your organisation.

Needless to say, business-imposed, work-related targets must not become a stick to beat your people with day in and day out. That is a shortcut to increased absence and attrition frankly. A light touch, informal daily catch-up is all that is required in most cases. A more formal approach to communicating actual performance compared to agreed annual objectives should be taken at monthly 121s. This will allow the employee to fully understand where they stand in terms of achieving their mutually agreed goals… leaving no room for unpleasant surprises come annual appraisal time.

Third, know and share all of your most important numbers daily. Create a 'dashboard' at agent and team level which clearly shows both your team members and your line managers how well each individual and the group as a whole are performing and progressing.

Dashboards are great for displaying key results in simple graphic and numerical forms which allow the viewer an instant snapshot of day on day/week/month performance. Stick to high level views of the KPIs which form part of your team member's objectives: quality scores, schedule adherence, AHT, sales etc. This document then becomes the basis of your daily chats and formal monthly 121s. You will also have all the uncontestable data you require at your fingertips ready for formal appraisal time.

Keep things simple. Use an existing Excel™ template and steer clear of complexity. Block off some time daily to update the data manually until you know how to pull everything you need automatically from existing sources …this is luxury as all of your reports will then be updated for you overnight freeing up more of your time to spend with your people.

Always be thinking about how you can move your focus from 'stuff to staff' meaning it's what you do on a one-to-one basis with each of the people in your team that will drive the best results. Concentrate on building productive relationships with the guys you manage rather than wasting time on reinventing an existing pro forma or process. Leave that stuff to your colleagues who would much rather be administrators than staff supporters and developers.

Most importantly, find the words that effectively communicate to each of your direct reports your intention to ensure the performance management process is part of a helpful and supportive endeavour designed to put the employee and their aspirations at the heart of the relationship between your business and the staff who work there. It must form the basis of the roadmap that will lead both parties to success in the achievement of both business and personal goals.

5 HR RELATED THINGS

For many novice Team Managers the world of Human Resources will be an entirely new thing. It's unlikely that they'll ever before have had to concern themselves with employment law, absence and lateness policies, terms and conditions of employment, distribution of contracts, periods of probation, disciplinary hearings, agency temporary staff and much more. It's crucial that managers fully understand the part they will play in dealing with all of the above and that they develop a framework of accurate knowledge that they can apply to situations as and when they arise.

Please be in no doubt – this is a big old topic and one that you are simply going to have to get your head around.

To simplify matters I've split your likely HR/Line Management responsibilities into smaller chunks with a focus on the areas you will be spending most time on. So, let's start with something very close to my heart. If you can develop superior knowledge and skills along with a professional, business-like, empathetic attitude then you can have great success in the field of absence management. Make an impact here and you can literally change people's lives for the better while building the kind of strong, efficient and supportive organisation that most modern businesses aspire to become.

As ever, I suggest that you become firm friends with some people who know a lot more about the subject than you do and will have had experience of most of the HR related situations you may become involved in during your tenure as a TM.

It is very likely that your business unit will have a designated HR Business Partner whose role will be to support the staff in your area with everything that's HR related. Treat this person with great respect and make yourself available to support them whenever they need it. This mutually supportive relationship can become a very valuable one indeed and should be pursued respectfully and within limits (avoid stalking and becoming an HR infatuated botherer and pest please).

Also, is there a TM in your department who you like and respect and have trust in their judgement and experience? Great – ask for ten minutes of their time to tell them that you believe you have a lot to learn and that you would appreciate their support by allowing you to shadow them at a return to work interview/disciplinary investigation/formal hearing etc. Make a promise that you won't bombard them with lots of future requests for their time and support and that you feel that by watching them in action you will be able to begin to form a framework for how you will handle these set-piece situations as you progress in your new role.

No decent manager will refuse that request and you will learn much more, and more quickly, about how things work in the real world of people management than you ever will from any number of workshops and briefings.

I'm sure they will be glad of any offer of support you can give in return but be wary of accepting the role of scribe at any formal hearing they may be conducting! What at first seems like an innocuous and not particularly challenging activity can end up in hours of typing and rewriting not to mention the surprisingly exhausting act of having to accurately scribble down the notes during the hearing itself.

Take on the role of scribe once to allow you to experience what's involved then run a mile from any future requests for support of this kind is my advice to you!! There are plenty of less arduous and time-consuming ways you can lend your support to your colleagues.

Absence Management

It is reckoned that absenteeism from work is currently costing UK businesses in excess of £11 Billion each year. Almost half of that figure as a result of long-term absence. The expression 'long-term absence' normally refers to a period of non-attendance at work of four weeks or more but individual businesses may have different definitions. The terms 'long-term absence' (LTA) and 'long-term sick (LTS)' have become interchangeable in recent years so you should expect to hear both used in your workplace and take them to mean more or less the same thing. Bear in mind that there is sometimes a difference in how sickness related and non-sickness related absence is treated within organisations. Familiarise yourself with your company's definitions of both.

The price for the individual employee is equally high. Low self-esteem, anxiety, depression are all conditions that can result when someone finds themselves stuck at home or in hospital due to sickness or challenging home circumstances. Time away from a person's place of employment, their work colleagues and the stimulation of the tasks they undertake when they're there can erode their sense of wellbeing and cause untold damage financially as household income reduces to danger levels.

It is fundamental to your role as Team Manager to appropriately support team members during a period of absence and to create a set of circumstances that will best help to bring the individual back into the workplace in a way that is beneficial to both the employee and the business.

As I've already said, developing an effective but sympathetic approach to absence management must be a top priority for every Team Manager. Getting long-term or persistent short-term absentees back to work in a sustainable, supportive and non-threatening way takes time and empathy and will require you to liaise with both Human Resources and Occupational Health teams. Only a joined-up, inter-departmental strategy will yield the best results and you will repeatedly have to lean on the experience and knowledge of those professionals to guide you through what can sometimes feel like a bit of a tricky maze and occasionally a minefield of law and policy.

You will, no doubt, be required to attend HR workshops covering this subject. It's crucial that you attend these with an open and inquisitive mind. The topic can seem dry at first. Once you become involved in real world cases involving actual people with whom you have an affinity, you will begin to find that guiding a struggling colleague through difficult times at a point when their health will be the biggest concern to them can be fulfilling and rewarding for both parties.

Take a note to yourself to become a recognised absence management 'expert' within your management community. Get to know your company's policy like the back of your hand then get on-line and read everything that's ever been published on the subject. Remember to scribble down relevant phrases and points of interest and incorporate the best of them into your personal absence management framework and vocabulary.

Dealing With Short-term Sickness Related Absence

Your starting point is this – read and absorb your organisation's absence policy until it becomes second nature to you.

Next, develop your script for dealing with calls from your team members telling you that they won't be in work for their planned shift. What information must you take from them and which questions should you be asking? I expect there will be an existing pro forma (a form) for this kind of situation so get your hands on that. You will clearly need to know why they are unable attend. Also, are they planning to make an appointment to see their GP? Which medications are they expecting to take to improve the situation? If things don't sound too serious (headache, minor stomach problems etc.) are they able to come in for the second half of their shift when they may feel a little bit better? If they have not followed the recognised absence reporting process then you must remind them of what that is as they will have covered it during induction training.

I'd like to raise some practical points at this juncture as I think it's important that you get an idea of the kind of tone you should be aiming for on these types of calls.

Naturally you want to be sympathetic and supportive so never stray far from that position. However, you must also get the message across that, as the person's manager, you are now going to actively manage the absence on behalf of your organisation and do everything possible to 'help' the caller to get back into the office and on shift as soon as they are fit to do so. You must maintain professional and business-like standards throughout and not become complicit in almost promoting a continuation of the time off that is being taken. By that I mean do not give the impression that the agent isn't really being missed and that they should take as long as they want till they feel 100% fit to return as this could easily and unnecessarily turn a one day absence into five days and you could find yourself short-staffed and struggling to hit service levels.

Some employees will perceive manager sympathy as permission to extend a period of sickness absence and may not make the required efforts to get back into the office as early as they could have done.

Finding the balance between genuine sympathy and the needs of the business – that is, to have as many staff as possible available for work - can be really difficult to achieve at first.

Believe me, it's hard to show sympathy when you receive a call on a Sunday morning from an individual who already has a track record of 'phoning in sick' at weekends telling you that they won't be in today as they have an upset stomach and are feeling nauseous. You also know that on Friday the same person had been talking about heading off to a big away match that the team they support was playing on Saturday and that he was planning to make a day of it (euphemism for having a large number of alcohol based refreshments).

Inevitably your suspicion will be that this is just another example of someone who had no intention of honouring his Sunday shift. It's also very easy to take this as personal insult – seeing someone deliberately trying to make a fool of you as their TM. Be very careful of your next move if you begin to feel that way.

Mentally congratulate yourself that you predicted this absence as soon as you were aware that the guy was planning to travel on Saturday. But, it is paramount that issues like this are dealt with through your organisation's formal disciplinary policy if the situation demands it. Never fall into the trap of venting your emotions at the caller even if he had had an earlier request for a day's leave rejected and you felt this call was always going to come. It's tempting but I wouldn't advise the kind of response that might sound a bit like this:

'Come off it Stevo I know you travelled to London for the game yesterday. You're either stuck down there or you've got a hangover and can't be bothered coming in. Which is it? Don't try to play me. This is the fourth time you've done this in the last six months. Didn't you put in a holiday request for today that I told you I had to reject because we looked tight on numbers?'

If this is in fact the fourth sickness related absence of this kind in three months it's likely that a threshold will have been crossed and an investigation will have to be arranged on the employee's return to look into the circumstances. Disciplinary action would then follow if appropriate. Any attempt to call the agent out like the example above could easily lead to a grievance being raised against you for the unprofessional way you handled his call as well as the fact that you seemed to imply dishonesty on his part. An unnecessary and complex mess would have been created when, frankly, just following the agreed company process would have done the job pretty well. Getting personal and implying scepticism when handling absence calls is a dangerous and potentially unfair business. Follow the agreed process – force yourself to do things properly at all times.

Professionalism means doing the right things right at all times!!
Recording and Documenting Absence

It's crucially important that all absence is reported immediately and accurately. As TM you will be charged with updating HR records and informing Payroll when an absence begins and when it ends. You will also keep a record of planned leave (holidays) in the same space.

It's likely that all of this can be done using your company's proprietary or bought-in software. Each organisation will have a different name for it but some of the most common suppliers are Ceridian, Kronos and Oracle. All look slightly different but do more or less the same things.

You must learn how to open and close absences as well as keep details of the reasons for absence. Fit notes and relevant correspondence will also be able to be stored there electronically which means there's less opportunity for paperwork to go missing. The system will then tell you when an employee's failure to attend has triggered a breach of the organisation's absence policy and allow you to plan for the next appropriate steps. A fully integrated application will also print out and store the formal letters required to invite staff to hearings and investigations as well as the paperwork necessary to communicate outcomes, warnings and dismissals.

Failure to keep the system up to date can prove catastrophic. For example, I've seen many situations where a TM has neglected to open and close an absence appropriately which then led to employees being significantly underpaid or overpaid as Payroll determines salary payments having first looked at the number of days worked recorded in the HR/Payroll system.

If a manager doesn't open an absence correctly then the absentee will be overpaid as Payroll will not know to deduct the number of planned hours not worked from their calculations. If a TM fails to close an absence then the application will tell Payroll that the employee has been not been at work even though, in actuality, he may have returned some time ago. He will then be significantly underpaid to the extent that he may not be able to afford to continue coming to work.

In these situations the incident will often have to be escalated to senior managers to sort out as requests for deductions and ad hoc out of sync payments may have to be made. As most people simply spend what they are paid, any attempt to claw back an overpayment made due to TM error will be met with a certain amount of animosity and ill will. Special arrangements will often have to be made whereby a percentage of the amount being reclaimed will be deducted from future monthly salary payments until the full amount has been repaid. Occasionally an employee will leave the business altogether rather than make a repayment leaving Payroll and HR to the very difficult task of trying to get money back from a what is now a former employee.

As you can imagine, employees who have to experience this kind of inconvenience through no fault of their own will very quickly lose respect for the manager whose error has caused the issue. I've seen good agent/manager relationships completely destroyed by this kind of mistake. Grievances have been formally raised and managers hauled over the coals all because they failed to take two minutes to make an entry into the on-line absence reporting system.

Even when all the correct processes are followed there can be Payroll challenges caused by dates of absence.

Most businesses have monthly Payroll cut-off dates. These are usually around the 21st of the month and are in place to allow the payments team sufficient time to prepare a staff salary run without having to make a large number of further adjustments. What this means in practice is that no salary deduction will be made in that month for any absence opened and closed after the cut-off date. The appropriate adjustment will take place in the following month's salary calculation.

An absence opened before cut-off that is then closed after the 21st will also not impact that month's payment but, again, any required adjustment will take place in the next month.

I know this can sound pretty complicated but, in reality, things usually work out alright as the majority of businesses will normally continue to pay permanent employees who have successfully completed a formal period of probation for a short-term absence of up to a few days. This probably won't apply to monthly paid temporary staff (agency temps are often paid weekly so problems can be dealt with almost immediately) or new staff who haven't yet completed probation however so it will be your job to spot when the salary of one of your team may be impacted then take time to explain how any over or under payment will be addressed.

It should also be said that Payroll departments will often allow a couple of days grace after the formal cut-off date for minor adjustments to be made assuming you ask them nicely and don't make a habit of it. Don't be annoyed if they can't help you out however as they will have masses of work to do between cut-off and the monthly salary run and may simply not have the time to go into the system and make the changes you need.

I'd really like to offer you a few suggestions here that can prevent you from making the kinds of payroll/absence reporting related errors that can cause real pain to people who need every penny of their salary to support them between monthly pay cheques. Here goes:

1. Input an open absence as soon as you have been notified of it.
2. Input a close of absence as soon as the employee has returned to work.
3. Get a list of Payroll cut-off dates for the next 12 months. Pay special attention to November and December dates (normally earlier in the month than the rest of the year) as any errors from you can ruin a family's Christmas.
4. Set automated diary reminders to notify you of any open absence that you feel may need to be addressed around cut-off time.
5. After weekends off or any period of leave make sure that absences from within your team have either been input on your behalf by another TM or have been reported to you by your buddy Team Manager to allow you to input on your return.
6. When planning to go on annual leave prepare a handover document for your buddy TM and have a meeting to take her

through all open absences that may have to be closed off before your return.
7. Meet with any adviser whose future salary payments may be affected by a recent absence and explain the nature of the impact and manage their expectations around deductions and overpayments.
8. Get yourself a friend in the Payroll department who you can very occasionally call or email to ask to sort out a salary payment emergency on your behalf.

So, there you are. The timely and accurate recording of absence is of paramount importance to both your employees and your business. It can be a bit of a minefield so take the time to learn all aspects of what will be required of you and build in fifteen minutes to your daily schedule for you to do nothing other that absence administration.

Long Term Absence

Your organisation will have its own definition of long term absence (LTA) but it usually refers to a member of staff being absent from work for a period of four weeks or more due to physical, mental or emotional ill health, injury or recovery.

As line manager your priority will be to support the adviser and help them get back to work as soon as possible. My advice is to see this as a dual role. The first aspect must be to manage the absence from work and the second will be to handle the agent's return to work. Getting on to the front foot and taking control of the situation should be a priority for you.

An initial 'I'm here to help' conversation with the staff member will offer you the opportunity to deal with any concerns the absentee may have and give you the necessary insight into the nature of the absence. Any medical evidence will provide a basic formal description of the nature of the underlying condition and perhaps a prognosis relating to the likely stages of recovery from which a rough estimate of the amount of time required before a possible return to work can be gleaned. This would also be a good point to find out from the employee how she thinks her employer could be of help to her and to introduce the concept of a referral to the Occupational Health as a starting point.

How you introduce and describe the function of Occ Health will go a long way to determining the absentee's future attitude towards that service. It is imperative that the employee perceives OH as being 'on their side' and that the focus of any dealings with them will be based on a mutual desire to maximise her wellbeing in her place of work. An Occ Health referral is not part of an employer's master plan to fast track someone out of their business – the truth, in fact, is quite the opposite. They are there to provide a health and safety framework for both employee and employer that protects both parties sufficiently to permit and promote a comfortable return to the staff member's role when it is deemed medically safe to do so.

It will be down to you to plan and communicate the next steps. Constant liaison with your internal stakeholders (HR/OH/Your Line Manager) and the absentee should provide all the facts and background information necessary to maintain an element of control of the situation. Case reviews should be diarised to take place every two weeks and formal conversations should take place between you as TM and the absent team member ahead of these sessions. Formal notes of each of these conversations should be taken – including dates, times and methods of communication - and must form part of the case file.

It may be necessary to meet with the absent staff member and this should be encouraged as face to face sessions often deliver better outcomes than a standard fortnightly telephone call when more or less the same conversation takes place and rarely moves anything forward. Rather than insist on the meeting taking place in the office it can be beneficial to suggest a 'neutral venue' like a café near the employee's home. In these situations take care to ensure your very private conversation cannot be overheard as this can impact on freedom to speak openly and the opportunity to build the kind of relationship that drives positive forward movement will be lost.

If the employee doesn't feel fit to meet you outside their home then – after guidance from your HR Generalist – suggest a home visit. This would involve you and another manager or member of the HR team visiting the agent where they live to discuss the absence situation and determine what the next steps should look like.

These kinds of visits can feel pretty uncomfortable when you're doing them for the first time. You will see your team member, someone you thought you knew well, in a completely different context. Their home may be grander or less salubrious than you expected and their behaviours are likely to be different to what you are used to seeing in the workplace – especially if other family members are around. They may appear distracted if they have small children in the room and you will generally feel like you're intruding on a part of someone's life that is nothing to do with you.

It's important to remember why you are there however. Your support can get them back to work and help to sustain the warm family life you've just intruded upon. A short, empathetic home visit can move things forward quickly if approached in the right way by both parties. It is imperative to come away with the next steps mutually agreed and for the employee to feel that having you in their home hasn't been an unwelcome intrusion. It also never ceases to surprise me the extent to which a colleague may open up to you at home in a way they just wouldn't in the office.

Very occasionally you will be confronted by an angry partner who does not approve of you or your visit to their home. Be prepared for this by discussing with an experienced HR staff member the possibility of such a response and take advice on how to deal with it.

Bear in mind the need for confidentiality as there will be aspects of the discussion that should not be witnessed by a third party if not deemed appropriate. I recall being thrown out of an employee's house by her angry husband when I told him that I had to speak to his wife alone due to rules around employee confidentiality. In retrospect I should have pre-empted this with the employee ahead of the visit by suggesting that some of the discussion would be private and that she could share what she wanted with her husband once the visit was over.

Home visits are very useful but it can be a difficult balancing act to try to be effective without disturbing the privacy of a family environment. Take lots of HR advice and make sure you are accompanied by a sympathetic figure who will positively contribute to the atmosphere rather than turn up as a pair of men in suits looking uncannily like a couple of detectives or debt collectors.

Always send a letter or email well in advance of the planned meeting to let the employee know when you will meet them and who will be accompanying you then phone ahead on the day of the visit to let them know you are on your way. I know this will give the employee a last-minute opportunity to take cold feet and cancel the session but it also allows you to confirm that they will be at home and that they are expecting you.

Unconfirmed appointments often result in the employee not being at home when you arrive at the agreed time and that just means more work for you as you'll have to track them down, find out why they weren't home as agreed and start the visit process all over again.

Return To Work

When a staff member returns from sickness absence they should be invited to a 'Return To Work' interview with their line manager or buddy TM whose responsibility it is to carry this out on behalf of the absent manager.

The purpose of these sessions is to establish a conversation with the employee about the reason for the absence, the nature of the condition that caused it and the future impact – if any – the condition may have on the agent's ability to work in his current role. It's also crucial to consider any workplace adjustments that may have to be made to support the individual as he gets back into the daily rhythm of taking forty calls a day from often challenging customers.

Your company will have a standard form for you to complete and store. Take time to fill in all sections and record all relevant detail including doctor's advice and medications prescribed as this information may have to be taken into consideration at a future date should the person require support from you, your management colleagues and your business as a whole.

Don't fall into the trap of turning the Return To Work process into a tick box exercise – something that you have to go through for process sake and because your HR policy tells you to. When a Team Manager takes a genuine interest in why a team member is persistently absent they may find themselves in a position (alongside HR and Occupational Health) to make a positive impact on that person's working life through the development of a deeper relationship between line manager and team member. Future absences can be avoided while on-going persistent absence related situations are prevented from developing where dismissal or resignation becomes the only option likely outcome.

Ensure that all RTW interviews take place on the day the employee returns to work. Don't put things off. The impact of a well-intended, considered intervention will be lost if you leave things a few days. If you know you're going to be on leave when one of your team is due to return make sure you've arranged with your buddy TM or the duty manager to pick the interview up on your behalf.

Should a repeat absence threshold have been crossed, or you have concerns about the nature of any of the information you glean from an RTW interview, it is probably a good idea to drop a note to your HR business partner and ask for their advice on how to proceed. If you have serious concerns that anything you learn may impact on the day-to-day operations of your department or business unit you should let your line manager know. It's better that she is kept in the loop in case HR feel the need to raise the situation with them at any point.

Medical Evidence

When a colleague is off sick for more than seven days they will be required to provide you with a Statement of Fitness to Work…..more commonly known as a 'Fit Note'. This will be supplied by a GP or hospital doctor after they have decided whether the employee is fit to work or not. If appropriate the doctor will advise that someone may be fit to work but that some adjustments to their usual role may have to be made. If that person is not fit to work then the note will make that clear.

It may be possible to accommodate a temporary change of role for a returner. For example, if an agent is not fit to take phone calls due to throat or voice issues you may be able to offer them on-line chat, social media or administration duties that don't involve speaking. If no such accommodation can be made then the CSR will be considered as unfit to work.

A doctor may also suggest a phased or gradual return to work or even a temporary change of hours. If you find yourself involved in any such situation take time to make sure that any change is documented and shared with the employee and HR and that formal review dates are built into the agreement. New equipment such as specialist back-support chairs or large format monitors and keyboards may have to be acquired in advance of any proposed return following an injury or medical procedure related absence.

There will be times when you, as a manager, may feel that the adjustments being suggested are out of proportion to the value of the return of a member of staff who may not have contributed a great deal to your business in recent times. Please bear in mind that as long as the proposed adjustments can be defined as 'reasonable' your organisation has a legal obligation to make them. Any failure to do so that leads on to the employee later leaving the organisation could result in a charge of constructive dismissal. A legal claim or employment tribunal resulting from such a charge could prove very expensive indeed should you be on the wrong side of the eventual outcome.

The financial cost could be significant enough in itself but the cost to the reputation of your business should the local media decide to pick up on the negative aspects of the story could be a great deal worse.

A team member can return to work before his fit note runs out. As his employer you must formally agree this and satisfy yourself that he is indeed fit to return. Keep yourself right by speaking to Human Resources would be my advice in this situation.

It's very important that all medical evidence is copied and kept on record either digitally or as a hard copy. Needless to say, every precaution should be taken to ensure the security and confidentiality of all such documentation.

Absence of less than seven days would be addressed using a process known as self-certification where the absentee completes a form detailing the reason for the absence.

Statutory Sick Pay

When a member of your team has run out of contractually agreed paid sick leave they may then be entitled to SSP. Study your company's rules on sick pay in detail to understand at what point contracted sick leave payment ends and SSP begins. Every business has its own rules around this.

SSP is a form of minimum sick pay that may be paid by an employer to a contracted member of staff who earns at least £480 per month and has been absent through sickness for four full days or more. Entitlement to SSP ends after 28 weeks and won't apply if the employee is already receiving statutory maternity pay or maternity allowance.

The current weekly rate of SSP is £95.85 but will increase annually by the rate of inflation or thereabouts. Employees must tell their employer that they are unable to work and are requesting SSP as no contractual sick pay is due. They must follow all relevant standard absence reporting rules in order to be considered for SSP.

SSP administration can be a bit of a minefield for line managers. Team Managers must take care to apply the same discipline to the management of an absence where an employee has moved into SSP territory as they would to a situation where the individual is still receiving full pay as stated within their contract of employment.

I've seen TMs become overly relaxed around ensuring the absentee is complying with the rules around fit notes and when to call to speak to a line manager about their continued absence. It's almost as if there's a feeling that the employee has moved into a 'lesser' category of non-attendee and has become more of an HR problem than a valued team member who must be supported back to work in a mutually beneficial way.

The cost to the business in purely cash terms of a short-term SSP absence may be lower than when a person is receiving full contracted sick pay but the amount of potential revenue lost is exactly the same. Paid 'holiday' leave entitlement accumulates as normal when an employee is absent through sickness.

Maternity Leave

Any member of your team who is pregnant is entitled to 52 weeks of 'mat leave'. This comprises of 26 weeks of ordinary maternity leave and 26 weeks of additional maternity leave.

During this period, requests for adjustments to normal working arrangements should be considered in support of any planned return to work. This could be a phased return from part-time to full-time hours across a number of weeks or an alteration to the usual shift pattern in support of the employee's new family circumstances. All reasonable requests for adjustments must be considered.

Staff who are pregnant or are on mat leave have a whole range of additional rights that are enshrined in law and must be taken into consideration when a line manager is offering support. I'm pretty sure you will be invited to an HR led workshop covering the subject in much more detail than I can here but spend some time familiarising yourself with both your company's policies and the law of the land as they relate to how a woman who is pregnant or on maternity leave should be treated in the workplace.

Please bear in mind that fathers also have rights in terms of paternity leave. It's crucial that you are familiar with guidance around these and build any potential paternity based time off into your future planning.

I'm not suggesting this purely so you can make sure you keep your actions as a manager on the right side of the law – this is important but not the best reason for taking time to learn how best to support a member of your team who will be going through a very exciting but sometimes tiring, challenging and uncertain period. You must become a help rather than a hindrance – create a smooth path through the work related elements of your employee's concerns rather than put unnecessary obstacles in their way.

Disciplinary Process

Unless you're some kind of sadist the handing down of sanctions to colleagues can be one of the least pleasant aspects of the Team Manager role. Sitting in a room surrounded by independent witnesses speaking in pseudo legal lingo terms to a member of your team who you were laughing and joking with about football and their less than healthy lunch choices just half an hour earlier has always struck me as unnecessarily forced and not a little OTT. A bit like pretending to be your school headmaster giving a life lesson to an unruly student.

However, making sure your organisations' policies are adhered to and that persistent flouting of the rules is addressed are fundamental aspects of the role. It's only fair to the business and wider staff community that transgressions are dealt with appropriately. Bear in mind, though, how you apply the disciplinary process and sanctions – when required – can bring positive results and shouldn't be perceived exclusively as some form of punishment exercise.

Usual starting point for the novice Team Manager – learn your company disciplinary policies and processes until you are expert. Become more knowledgeable and expert than every other TM irrespective of their experience. Only then can you become sufficiently sure-footed when planning and effecting your disciplinary interventions and dealing with HR on the subject.

There's a lot to learn here. Every aspect of the process is made up of seemingly endless sub-processes and there's a ton of administration that runs alongside each and every step. You'll need to get a handle on which formal letter templates to use and when…..legally determined notice periods abound here. Get your head around what differentiates an 'investigation' and a 'hearing' together with what constitutes informal and formal. Who can accompany the subject of the disciplinary hearing and who can't? Which room is most suitable to book for the meeting and which should be avoided (possible interruptions or the potential for being overheard by other staff). Which manager will accompany you as scribe and when will you be in a position to share the typed notes covering what was said?

All parts of the meeting process must be administered according to formal pre-determined guidelines. Attendees must be informed of how the session will be structured and how the outcome will be delivered. Meetings will introduced and concluded exactly as prescribed by company policy. Attendees must be informed that they can request a break as can the facilitator as and when required. Outcomes – including sanctions – must be delivered according to strict guidelines and the appeals process outlined. An opportunity to ask questions or seek clarification must be offered as a matter of course. It'll take you a while to get sufficiently used to the format and formal wording for all of this to start to become second nature to you but, when you do, meetings will flow naturally and you will become progressively more comfortable with your performance.

So much for all the policy process related stuff. Let's take a look at how you might think about facilitating the process and leading meetings in a human way that gets the best possible results for the business and the individuals whose behaviour you are now scrutinising.

The outcome of a disciplinary investigation or hearing must never be pre-empted. You simply cannot kick off the process with your mind firmly made up one way or the other. It's all too easy to be influenced by an employee's previous record of behaviour or simply what you think of them based on how you see them acting day to day. You've got to try to put all of that to one side and keep an open mind as you consider the facts and objective evidence relating to the case.

Maintain a professional but human demeanour throughout the process. Try to help the employee relax without influencing or unwittingly steering towards a particular outcome. Don't give the impression you are taking one side or the other. Treat everything they say seriously and don't immediately dismiss outlandish claims or excuses. Respect must be paid to all parties if the case is to be concluded without concerns being raised about your attitude and approach.

Sometimes it's difficult to hide your personal feelings – particularly in instances of possible gross misconduct. I once heard a case concerning one of my operations managers where he was accused by a TM of verbally abusing her at an off-site work-related social occasion. I didn't like the guy – I had inherited him when I took over the site and frankly, I would have been glad to see the back of him. I'd been told of his history of verbally abusing colleagues after he'd had a few drinks but I couldn't let what was really just gossip influence a decision that could potentially have destroyed the guy's career. I could also see how distraught the TM had become as a result of the whole affair. She threatened to leave unless the OM was dismissed but I couldn't let that influence my decision.

Having said all that I really didn't like the guy. To me he appeared lazy, smug, sneaky and at times downright insolent. A charge of gross misconduct with me heading up the disciplinary process was an opportunity for me to be rid of him once and for all. Everything about the guy irritated me. His over confidence throughout the process combined with his total disregard for the wellbeing of the TM he was accused of abusing really bugged me. He even turned up to the hearing accompanied by a very senior manager from another part of the business as his permitted supporting colleague – a move that was clearly designed to intimidate me and the HR generalist I had supporting me and acting as note taker.

In the end there was so much independent evidence against him my decision was made easy. The extent of the sanction was a less simple point to reach. As confirmed by HR I could dismiss him or take him to a final written warning with close scrutiny of his future conduct to follow. I badly wanted him out the door but a part of me felt that I was letting my personal feelings influence the final outcome when, actually, this was the first time a formal complaint had been made about him.

I decided to go down the final written route and, as we had expected, he appealed against the sanction as he just couldn't accept that he'd gone too far. He lost the appeal and left the business a couple of months later to work with his pervious boss at a rival company – he just couldn't accept that he'd been in the wrong.

I failed to persuade the TM he had abused that I'd made the right decision and that she should stay and build her career. She also left the business shortly after the hearing and joined precisely the same company that her abuser would later move to just a few weeks later….you just couldn't make this stuff up. The contact centre world is a very small place indeed.

I'm glad I didn't sack him. It would have been spite and nothing more to head straight for the most severe punishment just because of what I knew about him through office tittle-tattle. It's really easy to let your personal feelings cloud your judgement in disciplinary situations. Try to recognise when this is beginning to happen and pull yourself back to a more neutral stance.

Allocating Leave

Just a few words here on the best way to deal with requests for holidays that will inevitably come your way – usually through an automated process.

My advice is to deal with any request immediately it comes through if that is possible. Total permitted leave for the call floor on any given day is usually calculated in advance by Planning. They will usually build in a 'per shift' aspect just to ensure that all leave isn't being taken from within one start-time group potentially leaving them short-staffed.

Let's say your business plans in 7% annual leave each day and that there is total agent staffing requirement of 200 FTE gross. They may convert this to total hours (200 x 7.5 = 1500) then calculate available planned leave hours as 7% of that (1500 x 0.07 = 105). So in this example, on any given day all TMs have approximately 52.5 hours of leave to allocate for each of two shifts.

You don't need to be a genius to work out that the TM who approves leave earliest will have the best chance of satisfying her agents' requests. Sitting on a request for a prolonged length of time will end in disappointment for your team member and potential bad feeling heading your way. Rejecting leave can damage friendships!!

Obviously not all leave requests will be successful and this is where you, as a caring and considerate Team Manager, will have to become creative. You must look at where you might find agreement for potential shift swaps or re-arranged rota'd days off. Do (legitimate) favours if necessary to get your people the days off they really want and you will certainly find yourself making friends and influencing people.

Emergency Leave

All of us have days when the unexpected happens. Our perfect plans are ripped to pieces when real-life intervenes. This applies equally to the members of our teams and ourselves.

Most people simply cannot be expected to have an infinite number of family and friends available to pick up the pieces when the neighbour upstairs floods his bathroom and brings down your ceiling or to look after your sick child when she wakes up covered in spots at 7am just when you're ready to leave the house to start an early shift.

As a manager, it's part of your role both to show sympathy and support for your team as well as work with your planning and real-time management people to move resource around to cover any staffing gaps that may have arisen as a result of the unexpected, last-minute absence.

This is all part of a Team Manager's day's work and you should expect to have to deal with these kinds of challenges every time you enter the building. However, just occasionally, you will begin to identify a pattern developing where an employee begins to repeatedly request emergency leave on particular days or dates and gives the same (or similar) reasons for not being able to come into work. This is where your instincts have to kick in if you are to prevent a more threatening situation from developing.

Use the 'return to work' process to help you identify where an issue may be developing. Ask detailed questions about how a situation has arisen and get a sense of whether the same kind of thing is likely to happen again. Don't be afraid to make clear to the adviser that you have identified a trend and that you need to work with them to put an end to it. Explore ways for the employee to spot a potential problem in advance and make plans to cope with the circumstances in a way that would allow them to attend work as planned. You may have to help out by offering altered start and finish times or even reduce planned working hours but that is a price worth paying if it supports the employee in managing a tricky situation and allows you to deliver your team's total planned hours for the day.

If the interview throws up the need to find a solution to what may be a more permanent challenge for the team member (e.g. temporary loss of childcare etc.) then you should immediately inform Resource Planning and copy in both HR and your line manager to alert them to the work that you will be doing to attempt to find a mutually acceptable solution that doesn't end in the agent having to leave their role. As the planning guys have a better holistic view of what's happening across your business in staffing terms they may also present you with some potentially workable solutions. Don't be afraid to ask them!!

Remember that, in most cases, emergency leave will be unpaid. There's not much most of us can do when the real world throws unexpected last-minute problems at us but, when you spot one of your guys asking for this kind of time-off regularly, you can bet your bottom dollar that a bigger issue won't be far off. Losing three or four days' pay in a month can easily mean that the employee may struggle financially in the following month and this could exacerbate a developing issue further as time goes on.

Spot potential issues early and take immediate positive action - this must always be your intention.

6 PUTTING IT ALL TOGETHER

Let's face it – nobody really wants to have a boss. Seriously. Who, in their right mind, would want to subject themselves to the whims of some immature, under-qualified and over-promoted egomaniac for the entirety of their working life? 'Owned' like some kind of corporate servant by a patently unfit master.

Day after day of being told what to do then summarily criticised by the kind of person who should never be permitted to be in a position of responsibility for the very good reason that they always wanted to be 'the boss' in the first place. To my mind, anyone who aspires to have any kind of power over colleagues in the workplace should automatically be barred from even applying for any role that involves the management of people.

Yet we all grit our collective teeth and get on with it. We accept that some kind of line management hierarchy is probably necessary to help the businesses we work achieve their corporate goals while hopefully directing and supporting each employee's individual efforts. Underneath it all however, all we really need from them is the occasional pat on the back and the tacit agreement that we should be allowed to get on with things in the ways that suit us best.

So, assuming we absolutely have to be 'managed', what kind of manager do we feel we deserve? This can be a pretty subjective question but let me throw some of the usual adjectives at you: approachable, available, fair, supportive, emotionally intelligent, well trained, expert and 'professional'. But, what does 'professional' actually mean in the context of contact centre team management? What should you be aspiring to in your quest to become a recognised contact centre professional? Hopefully this will help.

How To Be a 'Pro'

As a starting point at the beginning of this really crucial chapter can we please agree on my somewhat simplistic but well intentioned definition of the term 'professionalism'?

For me, professionalism is simply a matter of doing the right things right – all of the time.

It doesn't matter what trade or industry you're in. Doing a few key things correctly at all times while avoiding careless errors should earn you the the much sought after accolade of 'true professional'. This matters because, underneath it all, if we agree to be managed at all then we each want to be managed by someone universally regarded a skilled professional. As individual employees we demand to be paid the respect of being taken seriously in the workplace by a serious manager dedicated to supporting our efforts and maintaining the highest possible standards.

I'm sure you're all too aware that the world of work is full of charlatans and pretenders who bluff their way through insecure volatile careers by pulling the wool over the eyes of their line managers and direct reports alike. They are almost always found out in the end but often not before significant damage has been done to businesses and staff who deserved better. They are the fakers who promise the earth and deliver very little. Do everything in your power not to fall into the trap of trying to fake your way through your working life. The unprofessional Team Manager creates discomfort, discord and dissatisfaction and leaves destruction in their wake. Much of this is often the result of laziness and a desire to take unnecessary shortcuts.

Operating Rhythm – A Key Concept

Being a pro in a TM role isn't easy. Literally hundreds of unavoidable distractions will be thrown in your path each day. You must learn to manage these while maintaining the unerring professional rhythm that guarantees the best outcomes for you, your business and your team members. There will be times when you'll feel that maintaining the highest standards is just too hard. After all, who's going to notice if you postpone planned coaching and team meetings for this month to allow you to focus on the new pilot project you volunteered for in an attempt to raise your profile with senior management? You will notice. And so will your team when their usual successful operating rhythm is disturbed. When the pulse of daily/weekly/monthly life in a successful group is disrupted eyebrows are raised and concerns for the future begin to emerge. A professional Team Manager will dedicate much of their time building and maintaining a full schedule of key support activities which should eventually take on a life of its own. When this point of self-propelling momentum is reached the expert TM will lay down her life to protect it.

What exactly do I mean by an effective 'operating rhythm'? Simple really – it's an established regular and consistent daily/weekly/monthly calendar of activities, interventions, interactions and events that add value to the aims of your organisation and the people who report directly to you.

It's the drum beat that drives the productivity and engagement of the group. When it exists it becomes part of the collective unconscious mind of any successful team. Everyone inherently understands what's expected of them and the part they play in driving positive outcomes. Each individual has an immediately accessible mental picture of when they must deliver their piece of the jigsaw and the minimum acceptable standards required of them. Team members have an almost instinctive grasp of what is planned for any time on any given day and have complete trust that their manager will enthusiastically deliver their side of the pact without distraction.

So, how do you achieve this fabled state of Nirvana? How do you reach a state of golden equilibrium where a team will almost manage itself and disruptive issues are rare? It's simple but not easy and requires extensive focussed and persistent effort in the areas of forward-thinking, planning, organisation, determination and influence. It can be hard work but worth it when everything comes together for you.

Ritualise Your Successes

The world's most successful rugby union international side, the New Zealand All Blacks, have a winning formula that promotes, perpetuates and supports continued present and future success whilst always venerating and celebrating the historical development of their existing methodology or 'Operating System' as I like to call it.

They are world leaders in consistently reviewing what works for them and what doesn't. Their proven ability to look for an extra 1% improvement, even when they are at the very top of their game, is legendary. They achieve this by first creating and embedding a unique culture or set of solid foundations upon which to build.

Keen observers have noted that a key tenet of the All Blacks' philosophy is defined in their often repeated phrase 'Ritualise to Actualise'. In simple terms this implores all players and staff to identify a very few, but-super important, habits that - when consistently applied by the entire team – combine to produce the best possible behaviours and, ultimately, results. They build trust in the group and support a sense of collective identity and purpose.

In New Zealand rugby terms these ritual foundations were often things like the obvious willingness for group leaders to 'get their hands dirty' and be prepared to do everything and anything they ask of their people, look for effective ways to change their game even when they they were winning, actively develop new leaders as they emerge, practice joint decision-making when appropriate and be prepared to sacrifice yourself for the betterment of the group.

Now, I'm not suggesting you attempt anything quite so heroic within your role as a contact centre Team Manager. I would ask you to lower your sights slightly and begin to develop a unique approach to three currently successful activities regularly performed by everyone in your group which you believe represent the core values of the team and should form the basis of the identity of the group. These could be:

- The nature, form and follow-up of your 121 coaching sessions
- The format and value of your live learning sessions
- The cool-headed approach to unexpected events and challenges
- The level of respect each team member demonstrates to others
- The positive collective approach to new projects and record of consistently delivering these effectively and on time
- The universal willingness of the group to volunteer for overtime and shift swaps when requests are made
- The desire to support and integrate new staff when they join the team
- Regular, fun, informal and enjoyable social events where all feel comfortable to attend

This list is endless. If your bunch of people is uniquely good at something then it's time to ritualise and embed the success. So, how do you go about 'ritualising' the good stuff in the workplace?

First, identify and define what your team is especially good at then give it a name that everyone in the team will understand. Make sure that the activity and the way it's performed aligns with your organisation's values and culture.

Second, ensure that the activity meets your individual and team objectives and doesn't obstruct what others are trying to achieve.
Third, regularise the format and diarising of the event to guarantee that it happens sufficiently often to class it as a ritual.

Next, make sure that you communicate the purpose, definition and regularity of the ritualised activity while outlining the part each team member will play.

Every society and culture has its own rituals. Whether it's weddings and funerals or religious or Summer holidays and birthdays we all have ritual-based milestones that help us make sense of our year. In almost all cases a celebration forms part of the ritual.

Simpler examples could be shaking hands when you are first introduced to someone, meeting your two mates in the same pub every Friday night at 8pm for a few pints or even the annual awards ceremonies many businesses hold at the same time each year to reward the best performing staff.

At a contact centre team-level environment I was struck by an excellent manager I used to work with who ran the most effective live learning sessions I have experienced. Her name is Andrea and she planned these thirty minute sessions to take place at the same time every week at a point she knew most of her people would be on shift but not on lunch or breaks.

The purpose of the session was always to cover off an element of call handling that was causing some people in the group issues in terms of delivery and understanding. The format was always the same: introduce and define the issue to be discussed, ask for comments on why some staff were struggling, play audio of good call examples then give those present the opportunity to discuss why these were good examples and which elements of the calls could be perceived as best practice and utilised by everyone going forward.

Andrea would then focus her next side-by-side coaching interventions on ensuring the agreed improvements were embedded throughout the team and on every relevant call.

Usually the subjects covered were simple enough to be covered in a thirty minute session but sufficiently important to drive call quality results upwards. Simple examples were how best to effect a customer's change of address, how to handle a security fail without upsetting the caller, how to word the beginning of an attempt to upsell…you get the idea.

What made these weekly mini-events different and added the ritual element, however, was not just the type of content or the format. Andrea wanted to make her weekly live learnings both productive and enjoyable so added a little five minute fun start to each meeting.

Each week one member of the team had to select their favourite biscuit and explain to the group why this was the case. Andrea would buy enough of these to share with the team before the meeting got started and people could bring a coffee or tea with them to complete the casual atmosphere.

Now, some of you will probably be thinking what I first thought when I heard about what Andrea was doing – something along the lines of 'yes, very nice little gimmick…what is all this biscuit rubbish actually going to achieve?'

Actually, it achieved quite a lot over the years.

The good-natured arguments over the choice of biscuit broke the ice and got everyone in the mood to talk about the best practice calls they would go on to listen to. Staff began to look forward to the sessions rather than dread them as just another attempt to criticise some peoples' call-handling skills.

Attendees could recall sessions weeks after they had taken place because they could tie the biscuit type and learning point together in their minds in a way that caused them a little pleasure rather than the pain of having to re-learn a key concept.

Other teams and TMs began to take notice and, once the usual cynicism was out of the way, new small-scale ritualised mini-events began to emerge from within the most forward-thinking groups and would eventually become part of the culture of the entire operation that was often trotted out as something we were particularly proud of when senior management and prospective new clients came to visit.

Andreas team suffered the lowest rate of attrition (agent turnover) across the centre and she consistently rated highest of all our Team Managers in 360 degree feedback surveys we ran every six months. This wasn't just because of the biscuit thing though – it was because she was the most professional, helpful, supportive and emotionally intelligent person on our books and we were lucky to have her...importantly, other less experienced managers began to copy some of her techniques and went on to develop into very capable professionals in their own right.

So, I hope you get what I mean when I talk about ritualising your successes. I'd like you to think about the things that are done well (or you are aspiring to do well) within your group then think again about how you can make this superior performance an innate trait that becomes so ingrained that it forms part of your team DNA. What can you do to conceptualise this successful attribute then run regular mini-events to advertise to the group and the outside world that you have something really good going on here and that people are having fun making it work?

Don't be too ambitious. Think small to begin with. The important thing is to make the ritual fun, regular and associated with the best possible behaviours and practice.

Get a couple of these right and you will begin to get noticed and appreciated for all the right reasons.

What Does a Professionally Managed Team Look Like?

First, think of an example of a dysfunctional team you've been part of or have seen at close quarters. Picture the constant disruption, controversy and melodrama, malicious gossip, unnecessary repeat issues and disillusionment the members of that team may have been subjected to. Did it look like a happy, productive and effective place to be?

Now imagine a very different team. This one is led by a Team Manager who consistently behaves professionally, with fairness and appears always to be in control – absolutely not a panic merchant. A team where every individual member knows what they are supposed to be doing at all times and has a clear view of what they are expected to achieve. They know, through good practice, when and where their weekly team meetings will take place and that these sessions will be valuable and enjoyable. The same applies to monthly 121s and annual appraisals – nothing gets in the way of these important interactions going ahead and any promised follow-up is completed and delivered within the agreed timescales.

Informal coaching regularly happens exactly as planned alongside the kind of formal training and development that helps everyone to do a better job and prepares them well for change to come. Opportunities for personal individual progress are communicated and fully supported by a manager who takes pride in the advancement of all of his charges.

Team members feel engaged and properly communicated with. Communication is genuinely a two-way street and everyone feels listened to and not simply talked at. They are trusted and respected. They are treated like adults and not kids. They feel like an integral part of the business they work for and have a genuine sense of value and worth. They are knowledgeable and well thought of throughout the organisation.

This is an environment where agents take the kind of pride in their work that ensures they will act as a professional, dedicated unit even in the absence of their highly respected TM. They also have fun.

I know what some of you are thinking – probably something along the lines of 'Come off it mate, this kind of perfection doesn't exist on call centre floors.' Or perhaps, 'I've been doing this kind of work for ten years and I've never come across a team or a manager who behaves like you've just described. Just doesn't happen.' I think differently. I can easily recall at least one standout team and manager that demonstrated the qualities and traits I've just described in each of the centres I've been part of over the last twenty-five years. Copy what they did and you won't go far wrong. By all means put your own spin on things and made appropriate adjustments but, if you follow the guidelines I'm just about to lay out, significant progress towards becoming a universally well- regarded professional manager running an effective semi-autonomous team will be guaranteed.

Contact Centre Team Management

Create a Weekly Structure

The first sign of a well-run team and highly-organised manager is a published defined structure to the working day, week and month. It doesn't have to be complex – just comprehensive and (most importantly) consistently adhered to.

Remember your school timetable? Well, that's the kind of thing you're looking for. My advice is to divide your month into four separate weeks and plan each week individually. Really simple. However, you must build in contingency for the large number of things that can spring up and interrupt your plans for the day and all planning must be done with the aid of your Planning and Real-Time Management teams as they will have a far better view than you of when high volumes of call traffic or planned training may impact your intention to remove your team or its members from the floor for meetings, 121s or coaching. I suggest you diarise a get-together with these support areas at the very beginning of every month in order to allow you to make the appropriate alterations to your team calendar as required.

I would suggest that you get all 121s completed within the first three weeks of the month and that weekly team meetings should take place no later than every Tuesday. The reason for this is straightforward; if events get in the way and these sessions have to be postponed you then have plenty of time to reschedule and leave the final week of the month free for a wash-up of anything that has been unavoidably delayed due to sick leave or planned holidays. There is no better feeling than having a 'free' week at the end of the month to allow you to catch up on anything that feels incomplete, increase your coaching and quality activity or support new or pilot initiatives.

Take into account also that if you are on an evening or weekend shift, access to your team members will be restricted due to some of them being on a different shift pattern to you. Also, as there will be fewer TMs on the call floor, you will be expected to deal with issues unrelated to your own team like handling escalated calls, dealing with senior management or client enquiries and the inevitable IT problems like phone lines going down and logins not working. Make sure you have plans and processes in place for dealing well with these kinds of interruptions but bear in mind that time with your own guys will be significantly reduced as a result of these activities.

This is also worth remembering – every time you leave your desk for a significant period you will return to find a request for support or information from some part of your business. For example, it is highly unlikely that you will be able to move smoothly from your 10am planned activity to your 11am session without the 'real world' getting in the way to some extent. The same applies when you come in to the office to start your shift…especially if you've been off for a couple of days. Always expect last minute priority requests to knock you off your stride a little. Build in contingency at the start of every shift and every hour of the day for unexpected interruptions. Help the guys in your team to understand that this will always be the case and that they should accept minor adjustments to planned calendar events. Communication will always be key in these scenarios.

Remember – teams react well to neatness, tidiness and clean and panic free organisation. Stick to the plan even if it kills you. Only make changes, adjustments or postponements if you have no other choice. Your monthly timetable of events should mostly be written in stone. Get your next month's meeting invites out at the end of the previous month and ensure that you have taken into account all planned leave (both your own and that of your team members).

Unplanned absence that gets in the way should be addressed on the first mutually available day – don't let anything drift towards the end of the month because, if unexpected events get in the way, the original planned meeting may never take place and you will start to 'get behind'. If you become too far behind you will become overwhelmed and both panic and stress will kick in….both of these states are to be avoided at all costs.

Find a Reliable Buddy

All Team Managers require a reliable and trustworthy TM buddy who can pick key things up in your absence. This really should be someone who thinks and acts like you and has the same dedication to ensuring all key events happen on time as planned. This will be a reciprocal arrangement meaning you will have to pick up some of their stuff when they are not in the office (remember to plan for this in your monthly calendar). This can sometimes feel like a burden but it's one worth taking on to ensure that your operating rhythm is maintained while you are on leave. You can take time off in the knowledge that you're unlikely to return to a pile of unnecessary and time-consuming issues that could have been avoided if you'd had a decent buddy in place. All absence will have been properly recorded as will leave requests and any urgent HR or performance related issues that require immediate attention. Sure you'll have to pick up all the follow-up work on your return but at least you won't be starting from scratch.

Get Yourself a Couple of Right-handers

What is a 'right-hander'? Put simply a right-hander is a member of your team who is entirely reliable, responsible and supportive and is keen to learn and pick up a small number of minor Team Manager functions in your absence or when you are going through a period where your time is short due to pressures from senior management or clients. Normally (but not always) a right-hander is someone who wants to learn the ropes of the TM role with a view to progressing their career. Sometimes they have no TM aspirations but just enjoy a little bit of variety in their day. No matter what their motivation is they should be people who are respected by the team and other TMs and who will definitely not leave a trail of destruction in their wake by disrupting relationships within the team or with the TM community.

Clearly right-handers won't have access to management level systems so wouldn't take on any of the HR type responsibilities but they should easily be able to support you in the preparation of call recordings for Quality Management purposes, do side-by-side coaching with the less experienced members of the team, handle escalated calls and ensure any potential 'people' issues are brought to your attention or the attention of your buddy TM if you are on leave.

It's crucial that you don't simply appoint your favourite team members to these development roles. This kind of perceived favouritism breeds all kinds of resentment and must be avoided at all costs if you are to maintain equilibrium within your team. Use your monthly 121s to determine who would like to try to learn more about the TM role and would be prepared to pick up some minor added responsibilities within the group. Give all appropriate and suitable volunteers a chance and create a rota that allows them to dip their toes into some basic support on your behalf. Those who perform best and you feel are the most reliable can then be used as your stand-in when you're on leave. That person becomes the eyes and ears of your buddy and maintains your operating rhythm without it being interrupted by your absence.

Again, it's really important that you don't reward the wrong behaviours. Anyone with a major absence or disciplinary issue should not be considered for further responsibilities until they have proved to you that they have cleaned up their act.

Keeping a Calm Head

During my time as a contact centre manager I've had to deal with telephony outages, network collapses, bomb scares, fire alarms, flooded call floors, a drugs raid by the police, staff walkouts, physical fights between staff members, colleagues becoming seriously ill and a number of other 'unexpected' incidents.

In the early part of my career when I was duty Team Manager at weekends and evenings I was terrified of something like what I've just listed happening on my watch. When it did happen I would panic and call everyone from the IT Director to the cleaning company just to ensure that I had covered all bases and taken all available advice. It wasn't a good look to be honest – the most senior manager in the building running around like a headless chicken trying to get help from anywhere he could. It was all so unnecessary.

The truth is that none of these incidents is unexpected. These things happen all the time and will definitely happen on your watch at some point in your future career. My advice to you is this – get a plan in place for every possible event on this kind. Familiarise yourself with the duty manager's handbook if such a thing exists and learn everything you need to know about your organisation's disaster recovery procedures. Keep all emergency names and numbers close both in your phone and on paper (remember if systems go down you may not have access to on-line intranet based information). Learn what do do if the first named emergency support individual is not available. For example, if telephony goes down and no-one in the centre can take calls and the named telephony support bod isn't picking up your calls, who are the next two contacts in line that can help you? Should you contact senior management or the relevant client to let them know what is happening in order that calls may be diverted elsewhere while you get the local issue dealt with?

Most importantly, assume an air of controlled urgency. Panic can be very ugly and infectious. You must appear to know exactly what you're doing and communicate continuously with all staff in the centre to help them understand the steps you are taking. Manage expectations realistically and don't be afraid to change break and lunch times rather than keep people seated doing nothing for a long period while you get to the bottom of the problem.

Remember this – the safety of the people in your building comes first at all times. Every decision you make should have safety at the heart of it. If that means calling security to help out with difficult colleagues or even evacuating the building if smoke has been seen coming from the canteen kitchen then so be it. Safety must come first – every time.

Try to bear in mind that all we really do is handle chat or telephone calls and losing a few of these is not a matter of life or death should things go awry. Doing the right thing for your people is what comes first and keeping a clear head and appearing to be in charge and in control should be your top priority.

Practice scenarios in your mind ahead of them becoming a reality. What would you do first? Who would you contact for help? Who would you gather around you to act as support on the floor? How should you summarise the event in a company-wide communication and who must you inform of your actions? How are you going to react to any criticism that comes your way the following day (as it inevitably will, no matter how well you performed during the incident)?

Please endeavour to always give off the impression of being in control and unfazed. You won't feel that way but it's crucial that all staff on duty see that they have someone in charge who has a plan. If you panic then many others will too and mistakes will be made.

On this page take a note of the five key lessons you've taken from the text of this book:

7 SUMMARY

Well, I promised you a *practical* guide to managing teams within contact centres and I hope that's what I've delivered. I've deliberately steered clear of management theory and science and tried to focus on the kinds of mini challenges you are likely to face every day at the coal face. Believe me, if you can get a handle on these and stay ahead of the game you will be far better placed to support your people, deliver business objectives and develop your career at a rate you would want for yourself.

I hope you've learned that little progress can be made without building strong relationships and getting the right people on-side. Your role is to help the people in your charge to become the best they can be and to feel good about themselves whilst delivering the quality of service demanded by both your customers and the business you work for. If you can achieve that, alongside supporting and promoting the efforts of the many departments and functions in place to keep large customer service organisations ticking over effectively, you can count yourself a success and a bright future will follow as long as you maintain the high standards you have set for yourself.

As usual, here's five points to take away with you. I hope they help to concentrate your mind and activity on what really matters:

1. ***Always*** behave professionally.
2. Select three to five ***people-based*** aspects of your role and become ***expert*** in each.
3. ***Work harder*** that every other manager.
4. Make as ***few enemies*** as possible.

5. Enjoy yourself.

Remember to put your people at the heart of everything you do and you won't go far wrong. At the end of every week take time to review what went well and what didn't and consider again how to focus better on 'staff' rather than 'stuff'.

8 TERMINOLOGY

All workplaces seem to have their own distinct vocabularies and one of the most difficult aspects of getting used to a new role can be coming to terms with the many acronyms, abbreviations and business-speakisms that everyone else seems to take for granted. Contact centres are worse than most for this so what I've tried to do in this chapter is give you some insight and explanation relating to the terminology you're most likely to come across.

They are listed in no particular order and I haven't covered everything you'll need to know and not all of what follows is universal across all centres and organisations. However, you'll need to familiarise yourself with this stuff and be able to use it intelligently if you are to be taken seriously in your role as Team Manager. Take care to learn how to use these terms correctly and in the right context.

Average Handling Time (AHT)
In simple terms this is calculated by taking the total of an agent's talk time in seconds and dividing by the number of calls handled. Total AHT is made up of talk and wrap time and is measured daily, weekly and monthly at agent, team and centre level. AHT is a key metric or KPI for planning staff numbers and costs and managing customer experience.

After Call Work (ACW or Wrap)
ACW covers the things that a call handler has to complete after speaking to a customer. So, updating a customer record or the reason for the call are examples of what would fall into this category. It's important to coach your team members to be as efficient as possible through finishing as much admin as possible while talking to the customer rather than waiting till the call is completed. This reduces ACW and overall AHT plus it allows more customer calls to be handled due to increased availability.

High ACW is often a sign that an agent is unsure of standard processes or needs support in learning how to talk and type at the same time. Occasionally it's because they don't fancy taking the next call and would prefer not to be available.

Erlang Formula

Agner Krarup Erland was a Danish engineer and maths whizz who created the first formulae for forecasting and managing queueing within telephone network traffic. Although analysis and theory have moved on considerably since his day (1878-1929), modern contact centre staff planning applications still use basic Erlang concepts to forecast required staff numbers. The formula takes total calls forecast, target SLA, AHT and ACW then calculates how many staff will be required to ensure that service level targets will be met.

Service Level Agreement (SLA)

An SLA is used for setting out how suppliers (internal or external) agree that a service will be delivered. This is usually a contractual measurement and normally – in contact centres - refers to what percentage of offered calls will be answered within a target waiting time alongside a maximum abandonment rate. Failure to achieve these minimum targets will often result in contractual service penalties which can seriously erode planned revenue.

So, as an example, an agreement could be that 80% of all calls offered should be answered within 20 seconds with no more than 5% of calls abandoned without being answered or forced to disconnect.

As shorthand this would be referred to as an SLA of 80/20/5.

Cost Per Call/Per Call Minute

In outsourcing contractual agreements the supplier will charge the client for their services in a number of different ways. Each method of charging carries with it a movement in the balance of risk from client to supplier. The most common methods of charging are cost per call or per call minute – although invoicing for each FTE and total productive hours delivered are also often used.

The cost per call model is simple in that the client pays the supplier an agreed amount for each call handled. The value of the call is determined by the contracted AHT and technical skill level required of the handler to deliver the service. For example, a 600 second AHT target technical support call will be of higher value than one that is 240 second in length and delivered by a customer service adviser.

Cost per call minute is very similar in that an agreed value is placed on each 60 seconds of the call rather than the call in total.

Full Time Equivalent (FTE)
FTE expresses total contracted hours expected of an individual employee as a factor between zero and one. Sorry if that seems vague but it's really very simple.

If full-time staff are contracted to work 37.5 hours per week then anyone working 37.5 hours will be counted as 1 FTE. Someone working part-time hours of 18.75 hours will count as 0.5 FTE. A part-timer doing 30 hours will go down as 0.8 FTE. Got it ok?

Be sure not to get confused between total FTE and total 'heads' or 'headcount' as they'll inevitably be different numbers if you have part-time staff within your group. The numbers will only be the same if you have exclusively full-time staff in your team.

Interactive Voice Response (IVR)
This is automated telephony that allows customers to feed in information to allow their call to be routed to the correct business area.

An example of this could be when a customer calls their credit card provider to pay a bill. The IVR will take the card number and other secure information before offering the opportunity to pay the outstanding amount automatically through speech recognition or using the keys of a phone or having the call routed to a live agent. Most organisations now prefer their customers to 'self-serve' through either IVR or interactive website rather than speak directly to an agent. The reason is pretty simple – telephony agents are expensive and talk is far from cheap.

It would be time well spent if you could ask one of your Telephony people to take you through the map of how your calls travel through the IVR.

EBITDA
Earnings before interest, taxation, depreciation and amortisation.

This is really just top line earnings before a bunch of costs are taken off. Also known as programme profit you are left with your operating profit number once ITDA are deducted.

C-SAT

Short for 'Customer Satisfaction'. This is usually measured in a survey or questionnaire which is sent to customers by email or text. In some cases call handlers will be prompted to ask random customers if they are happy to be transferred to an IVR based C-SAT survey to allow them to comment on the service they have just received.

In outsourcing this is often a contractual metric which can attract service penalties in the event of targets not being met.

First Call Resolution (FCR)

Companies will often measure how often a customer calls back with the same query within a short period of time (usually 10-14 days). The purpose being to determine if advisers are fully answering and dealing with a customer's issue.

If a caller has not had their questions and requests dealt with satisfactorily it is likely they will call to talk to a different adviser with a view to having their issue dealt with properly second time round. Repeat calls are expensive and must be kept to a minimum.

As a TM you will require IT and Telephony support to identify which customers have called back soon after having spoken to one of your team members. Your job will then be to listen to recordings of these calls, identify where your agent is going wrong then urgently create and kick-off an appropriate coaching plan designed to remove the faults that are leading to customers having to repeatedly call to speak to other more helpful employees.

Automatic Call Distribution/Distributor (ACD)

You'll hear a lot spoken about ACD. In essence it's the application or software and hardware hybrid that answers and routes incoming calls. It will intelligently deliver calls to specific business areas or agents within and organisation. The hardware element is often called the switch.

Voice Over Internet Protocol (VOIP)

VOIP is the technology that delivers telephone calls over internet networks rather than the more traditional 'telephone lines'.

VOIP is a less expensive and more efficient method of call transmission within contact centres compared to the traditional circuit method. Potential downsides are poor sound quality if too much compression is used and also the fact that all forms of comms are lost if the network goes down. Previously, telephony and IT infrastructure would be based on separate elements meaning that calls could still be handled by an agent even if the network his PC was connected to had failed.

Key Performance Indicator (KPI)
A KPI is simply a performance measure designed to put a number against how well, or badly, an organisation is meeting its objectives. Most common KPIs used in contact centres are AHT, SLA, Productivity, Occupancy, FCR, Shrinkage etc.

Shrinkage
This is a resource planning term and refers to the percentage by which total staff numbers are reduced due to planned and unplanned absence.

To ensure sufficient staff are on shift, staffing forecasts will begin with the net number of agents required to handle an assumed number of calls at any given time. Those numbers are then increased to take account of the amount of staff expected to be absent due to sickness, holiday and emergency or unplanned leave. So, if you expect 30% (shrinkage) of agents to be absent between 2pm and 3pm on Friday and you know you need a minimum of 10 people to be available to take calls then you must increase your required staffing by 30% to 13 for that hour as you are expecting 3 people to be absent.

Average Speed of Answer (ASA)
In short, this is a measure of how it takes for your agents to answer calls offered. You really want this to be a low number as this indicates that the team is being efficient in responding to delivered calls. High ASA might be a symptom of poor staff planning, high absence etc.

Average Call Wait Time
What it says on the tin. If this is too high then call volumes may be higher than forecast or agents could be taking overly long to react to calls offered. Long wait times lead to queues and unhappy customers.

Productivity, Utilisation and Occupancy

This is a tricky one because every organisation I've worked for has measured these differently. However, they are usually calculated by adding up call, hold and wrap time then expressing it as a percentage of logged in time.

Too low a number combined with persistently high availability and service level figures may indicate scheduling inefficiency......too many people on shift for a given call volume forecast. Too high an occupancy number will mean agents are being bombarded with calls with little time for them to recover from the previous enquiry before having to deal with the next. This leads to errors and potentially burnout. Optimal productivity/utilisation/occupancy should sit around 85% and it's up to your resource planning people to get their call forecasts and staff scheduling as accurate as possible to support this target.

Resource Planning

These guys are responsible for taking all the usual planning assumptions (call forecasts, SLA target, expected shrinkage, planned AHT, productivity etc) then producing manageable and efficient shift patterns and schedules. They are the people who determine how many staff in total are required to work on a campaign or project, what the part-time/full-time mix should look like, shift start and finish times along with when days off should be taken as well as fixing times for breaks and lunches.

Get to know this team and respect what they do – they have a truly challenging role. If they get it wrong it can detrimentally impact profitability and employee satisfaction. To get good results they must consistently balance a whole raft of factors and be prepared to make adjustments at short notice in an effort to meet changing senior management demands.

Schedule Adherence

Usually expressed as a percentage, this metric will tell you to what extent each of your team members is starting, finishing and taking breaks at the right times as requested in their schedule. A number in the low nineties could mean you have someone who is starting late or finishing early or taking breaks when they want to rather than scheduled. Check the daily login/logout reports to get a clearer picture.

Bear in mind that it is often impossible for an adviser to end a call exactly in time to start a break or lunch at the scheduled point in the day. Some non-adherence is therefore inevitable and allowances should be made.

Login/Logout Report
Familiarise yourself with this page in your reporting suite – it can tell you so much about agent behaviours.

The numbers on here will confirm when an employee began and ended their shift for the day alongside when they started and finished breaks and lunches (assuming your policy is to log out for these). Use it to let your wayward team members see evidence of persistent late logins and early logouts. Look out for multiple loggings out followed by loggings in with no more than a couple of minutes in between as this can point to call avoidance – in short, an adviser logs out rather than sitting in wrap so that they can avoid taking calls.

Call Recording
For quality, record keeping and compliance reasons it is likely that all of the inbound and outbound calls you handle will be recorded. Various platforms are used for this function and it's crucial that you learn how to access this application and to manipulate its search, playback and store functions to support your coaching efforts.

Nice, Verint and Genesys are the most common call recording solutions providers in the UK and it's worthwhile spending some time on line with a view to understanding just what their products are capable of.

Voice and Speech Analytics
Information can be extracted from voice calls by specialist applications designed to identify and extract specific, defined information for use in supporting improvements in customer interaction and relationship management. Using speech recognition technology this type of software can help managers understand process and performance weaknesses and act as an aid in coaching and develop

ABOUT THE AUTHOR

Kenny Gow has worked in senior contact centre management roles for more than twenty years and is fascinated by the challenges and opportunities presented by the recruitment, training and practical day-to-day management of the people who handle calls, chats and customer interactions of all kinds for a living.

Over those twenty years he has seen things done - and done things himself - both well and less well and is determined to save others from making unnecessary mistakes while offering a few pointers towards achieving accelerated and consistent success.

Printed in Great Britain
by Amazon